The New Ma'at

Origin of Egypt, Civilization and the Ten Commandments

by
Gabriel Senior Scott

Published by the Trustees of the Gabriel Gold Corp.
Copyright © 2020 All rights reserved.

ISBN-13:978-1727056839

Contents

	Preface	3
1	The Origin of the Mystic Kushite	10
2	The Myth of the Transcender	19
3	Historical Kush (Part 1) Were they black?	27
4	Historical Kush (Part 2) Kushite Uniqueness	32
5	Historical Kush (Part 3) Egyptian Anu-Kush?	45
6	Historical Kush (Part 4) Kush Manifestations	61
7	The Religion of the Kushite	77
8	Kushite Definition of Civilization	103
9	Kushite Art and Architecture	116
10	The Just Wars of the Kush	151
11	Kushite War of the Homeland	167
12	Continuation of the Cultural Rift	173
13	The Kushite Conquest of Egypt	181
14	Kushite Guardians of the Levant	189
15	The Persian Invasion of Egypt	197
16	The Kushite and the Greek	203
17	The Kushite Verses the Roman	210
18	The Kushite Warrior Queen	216
19	The Last Kushite Renaissance	225
20	Kushites, Christians and Islam	229
21	Race and the Ancient Kushite	235
22	Race of the Egyptian Pharaohs	251
23	Kushite Cultural Foundation	273
24	A Gift to the Diasporic Kushite	281

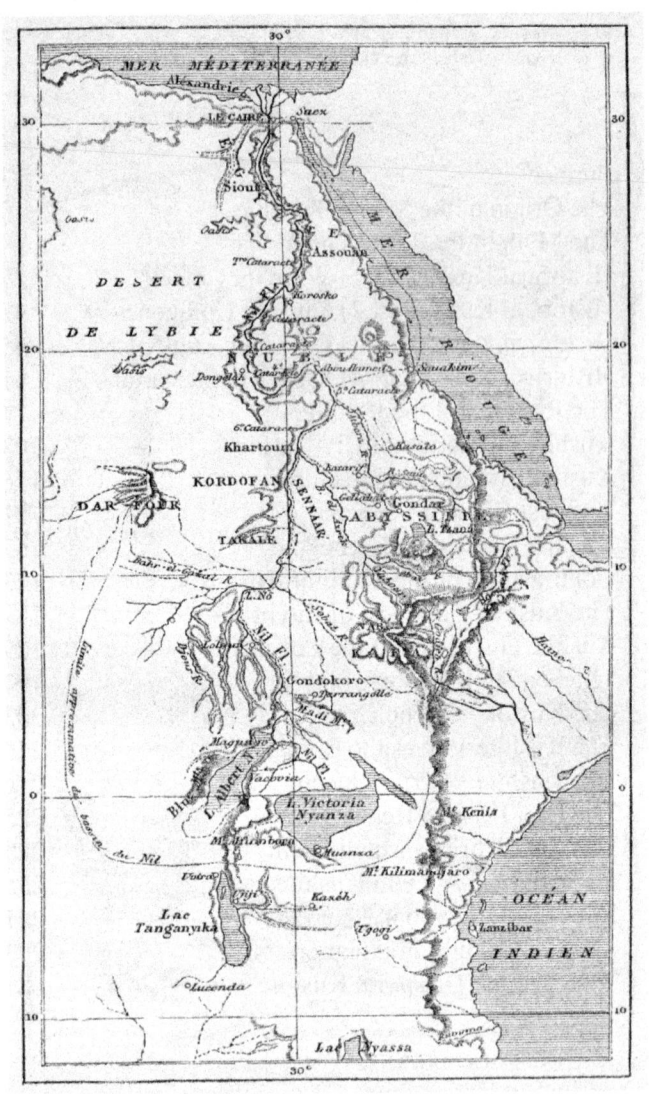

Old Map of the Nile Valley

Preface

It was the early evening of April 4th, 1968, when my perception of the world and its people changed forever. A Mutual of Omaha insurance salesman had dropped by my home to review a product to my mom. She asked if I could sit with her while the insurance guy explained the policy.

We had just gotten comfortable as the three of us set in the living room of my childhood home. Suddenly, there was an urgent news report flashed across the screen of mom's old black and white T.V. Set. Martin Luther King had just been assassinated!

I recall the enormous rush of anger flowing through my adolescent body. Being a teenage black male in 1968 was a dangerous business, and the enemy was well defined. I knew my enemy from the bitter rhymes of the Last Poets. I distinctly remember turning to the insurance salesman and saying in no uncertain terms, "get the hell out of my neighborhood, now!" A look of absolute terror flowed like an ocean's wave across the salesman's face, as he disappeared before my very eyes.

Mom's Kushite Decency

I'll never forget the outrage my comments to the salesman elicited from my mother. In no uncertain terms, she said, "How dare you speak to an adult in that manner. This is my home child, and only I have the authority to order someone out! Respect Gabriel, always respect." I didn't know it then, that my mom's harsh words were in-fact my first real lesson in the tenets of the Ma 'at. The pure shock of my mom's anger, which I had never experienced before, compelled me to offer an immediate and humble apology.

An Evening of Turmoil

The evening was quiet at first, but there was an undeniable feeling of impending danger in the air. Within hours, the rioting, looting, and street battles began just blocks from my home. The news indicated that violence had broken out all over the county.

I recall my youthful anger, which was tempered by confusion coupled with an unbelievable willingness to die for a cause I had yet to understand fully. As my mom and I sat glued to our black and white television, I could feel the world raging right outside my front door.

Later that same night, I asked my mom to explain this "race thing" to me. Until that day, race relations were never a focused subject in our household. I wasn't completely naive. I had undoubtedly noticed the induced poverty in my community, police brutality, and a sense of general white hostility to my people. I didn't know why, and it made little sense, given their brutal treatment of my people and many others.

It was my understanding that whites made us slaves, not visa-Versa. I righteously felt that it should be the victim, not the victimizer, who should express anger. For the first time, this made me see whites as an entitled and uncivilized tribe with a complete inability to recognize themselves.

Mom and I communicated that night in a way rarely repeated during my childhood. Many of the race stories she shared with me from her experiences in the south were both personal and horrific. However, there was one story mom told me that challenged my imagination.

Mom spoke briefly about the existence of a great and powerful black African civilization known as the Kushite. As mom began her story of the Kush, something in her changed. I saw in my mom's eyes what I know now to be the spirit of Kushkara, one of the first of the female Kushite Transcenders.

According to mom, the Kushites were the origin of the Egyptians and a highly advanced civilization. These powerful people also boast of influential female warrior leaders and a uniquely decent relationship to all humanity. I will never forget my mother's words. "I wish but one thing of you, my son. I pray that you will grow to be a strong and compassionate man of God and a warrior of human decency like that of the Kushite. Gabriel, to be a warrior of this type will require an astounding level of courage."

I recall thinking, cool, and not much else. By this point in our conversation, my mind was starting to drift away from revolution and back to girls. While I cared deeply for social justice and did what I could over the years, I was also in high school and far more interested in dating and gymnastics. Time passed, and the world moved on. All this Kushite non-sense would probably have ended on that fateful night if it were not for what came next.

The Beginning of My Obsession

In college, biology, medicine, genetics, and software engineering, which was beginning to emerge, were my primary interest. However, Kushite history became my part-time passion. Finding materials on the Kush back then was extremely difficult. Even on campus, articles on the Kush were rare. Lucky for me, I had direct access to an excellent black history department. Many of the professors and other associates helped me to develop techniques for extracting historical information about the Kush. What drove me were the continuing insults from the whites and the rhymes of the last poets echoing in my young mind.

"Understand said the old black man who is the opposite of you. Understand so you will know what you need to do. Understand that black is right, and white is wrong. That white is noise and black the song. That blacks will live in glory and whites will die in shame, that blackness is reality and white is but a game. Understand said the old black man who is the opposite of you. Understand so you will know what you need to do."

I have become that old black man mentioned in the last poet poem above, and I know precisely what to do! What must I do? What I have been doing all of my life! Expand my mind and speak the truth! Via the way of the Kush, I've come to realize that the problems plaguing humanity have never been as simple as black and white. Our human-induced problems are much more a question of right and wrong drenched in self-interest, inferiority complexes, false pride, confused identities, and situational morality. I've also come to understand that evil, not color, is the opposite of me. I will not hesitate to attack and destroy evil in all of its forms!

I Studied for Fifty Years

The information I will share with you in this text is a small sample of my knowledge of the Kush. A few of my favorite techniques for exploring Kushite history during my youth were historical references, migratory gene patterns, and expert interviews. Over the years, I have interviewed several African professors of history and Egyptology. However, the professor that most influenced my vision was Doctor Cheikh Anta Diop and Chancellor Williams. Doctor Diop is the author of the text "The African Origin of Civilization." Chancellor Williams is the author of the book "Destruction of Back Civilization." If you wish to dig deeper into African history, these two texts are an excellent start.

Doctor Diop was a slightly built professor of physics and an African historian who, for one week of my life, became like a father to me. Our conversations were profound as I witnessed the dynamic courage of a man shouting truth into an empty void. I wanted to be like Diop, and the history of the Kushite would be my path.

Professor Diop left us in 1986, but his legacy of historical truth will live forever in my heart. The insights I've gained from Diop's approach to history drove my interest in the Kushite for the next fifty years of my life. Doctor Diop's final words to me were, "we owe this historical struggle to our ancestors and to our children!" I do so wish he were here to read this book. I know he would share my pride in this modest endeavor.

A Personal Revelation

The deeper I delved into the Kush, the more profound the Kush became. I realized that the Kush that I was initially introduced to was far more significant a people than my mom and I could ever have imagined. Over time, I subconsciously incorporate Kushite thought and tradition into my everyday life. By studying the way of the Kush, I had become Kush.

The Kush provided me with purpose, discipline, and direction that resulted in a life well-lived. I sincerely thank my mom and the way of the Kush for my good fortune in life. My life has been a fruitful experience that may not have occurred had mom not introduced me to the unknown Kush.

I didn't realize until I began this book, just how much my quest for the Kush had influenced my entire adult life. The stories of the Kush changed my behavior, how I saw myself, others, and the world. The Kush encouraged me to master countless skills, despite my many deficits, because that was the way of the Kush.

My understanding of the Kush made me feel powerful and itching to fight the American culture wars while others hide from this reality. The Kush made me self-defining, courageous, confident, forgiving, respectful, ambitious, responsible, and even a little bit moral. The Kush gave me honest answers to the most challenging problems facing humanity. But what the Kush gave me most was something I didn't realize I had lost, my black African cultural continuity.

Saving the African Diaspora

The African diaspora of both north and south America was cruelly ripped from our ancient ancestry, causing a significant loss in cultural continuity. While it would be impossible to reverse the damage this disconnect has caused, it is not impossible to recover from the negative aspects of its existence. Knowledge of one's ethnic history is imperative for restoring the continuity of identity required for a productive future.

But what is the right culture to emulate when the diaspora is from many different origins? The answer to this question is the best cultural representation you can find. How many times have we heard western historical scholars pronounce that Egypt and/or Mesopotamia are the origins of western civilization? They make these claims even though neither of these cultures is European while denying the black African origin of Egypt. My argument is simple! If they have a right to make assumptions of this magnitude, then so do we. Western scholars have chosen Egypt or Mesopotamia because they were the best cultural representations they could find. Of the civilizations I have studied, both in and out of Africa, none come close to the Kushite. You are about to learn why!

Sadly, if I were to mention the word Kushite to a person of any race here in America, most would have no idea what I was talking about. Some might ask, do you mean the Kush from the Bible? Others will relate the word Kush to a strain of marijuana. Here we have a proud and independent African civilization that traces its roots back more than 8,000 years, yet they are nearly unknown to our society. This is not the fault of the whites; this is our fault!

In this text, I'm going to argue that the Kush was probably the origin of Egypt, civilization, and even the ten commandments. I use the word probably in order to honor the Kushite virtue of humility. I will argue that the Kush was a unique society based on morality rather than greed and dominance. I'm going to show you that the very definition of the word Kushite means the moral human being. Keep this definition in mind as you read this text, and you will come to understand what made the

Kushite so great.

The historical tragedy of the unknown Kush ends now! My training in the way of the Kush began 50 years ago and will be laid before you in this text. My mission is to reignite the cultural direction of the Kush, starting with the completion of this text. I want nothing less than to redirect the moral imagination of the African diaspora across this entire planet.

I will show the diaspora an alternative story based on fact, that I hope will become a unifying force among its many diverse members. I predict that the day will come when the diaspora will rise as one and shout the words of the great King Kushta. "I am Kush, the moral human being!"

The Kushite Warrior

Many of you will wonder why I sometimes use the term Kushite warrior in this text. You might mistakenly believe that warrior relates to weapons and strategies of conflict. While firearms and tactical strategies are essential, it's what you are inside that will determine the outcome of every battle you encounter in life.

Real courage in the face of overwhelming odds comes from a moral foundation. An internal code of human decency that will not allow you to ignore right from wrong or justice from injustice.

With this review of ancient Kushites you'll come to understand the fundamental importance of a moral path in life. You will learn that every decision you make in life has a moral component. You may also learn that there are higher values that are more important even than the preservation of self. The Kush understood this, which enabled their civilization to last for thousands of years.

Chapter 1: Origin of the Mystic Kushite

Created by the Hand of God

Thousands of years ago, in the cradle of mankind known today as Sudan, there existed a people created directly by the hand of God. These people were called the Amelineau (Anu) who are the black African ancestors of the Egyptians and the Kush. The Anu was different from all other people on earth because the origin God Amun and the Goddess Ma'at had given them an exceptional gift called virtue.

Because of the generosity and virtue of the Anu-Kush, the Gods granted them the secret to happiness, prosperity, and peace. But, to enjoy the fruits of this gift, every Anu-Kushite had to complete a secret process called Kushite Warrior training. Both genders had to complete certain aspects of this training that began at age four and could last a lifetime. The Kush believed that once the meaning of warrior training was understood, the warrior is prepared to do battle with and defeat the all-powerful minions of Chaos.

While warrior training may sound like the introduction to a video game, the outcome could not be more serious. The Kushites believed that the very survival of humanity depended upon each individual's ability to master warrior training, spelled out in the tenants of the Ma'at.

Lesson One of the Warrior Code

The Kushite possessed a remarkable book called the Ma 'at, also known as the Kushite doctrine of human decency. This text was the foundation of warrior training, and its first lesson was the most profound. You are both the source and the key to <u>harmony</u>!

Have you ever wondered where the soul of the unsung hero goes after death? I'm not talking about the decorated soldier who, by any standard, is our most valued hero. I'm talking about you, the ordinary moral human being. The one who without fanfare or appreciation works hard to assure your children have food on the table and a safe place to sleep. You who, by placing one foot in front of the other, strive to create a clean and just society. You upon which social harmony is dependent are the real warriors and heroes within the Ma 'at.

Many cultures believe that the soul of the good are elevated after death to the level of an Angel. Kushites believe that the soul of the warrior is eternal and can be passed from one person to another via the golden gene. The golden gene, also known as empathy, or the positive spiritual essence, is the most crucial weapon in mankind's war against Chaos. The Ma 'at makes it clear that he who possesses the golden gene is the most powerful warrior of all!

Kushite warriors fight for justice by fighting for one another. The moral Kush knows that our very survival rests on our ability to unite and defeat Chaos (evil or injustice). This battle cannot be won without dedicated warriors who place the good of the whole above the interest of self.

The Kushite is neither a saint nor a juggernaut. He/she is not smarter, stronger, or more courageous than any other human being. What sets the Kushite warrior apart is their dedication to the principles of justice and devotion to the greater good. A warrior's strength is derived from karma that flows directly to the righteousness of the cause.

Having virtue alone is not enough. Each warrior must be trained in the way of the Ma 'at (way of the Kush). The Ma 'at is the primary weapon used to defeat Chaos, and without it, you are left helpless and confused. I warn you, young warrior, that to see Chaos is to look upon the hideous face of evil. This horrible sight can be devastating to the weak and the untrained. The tenets of the Ma'at will guide you, providing the strength and knowledge you need to overcome any evil obstacle placed in your path. The Ma'at will protect you from despair and elevate your soul to the highest standard of Kushite tradition.

The Ma'at will enable you to recognize evil in all of its forms and allow you to wield the weapon of the golden gene. Upon accepting the awesome strength of this weapon, you will become Kush. Once you are Kush, neither Gold nor mortal threat will turn your heart from justice, and you will join the ranks of the invincible Kushite warrior. If you do not receive this gene, you will become the Apepa (servant of evil). Know this, an Apepa can never transcend. Upon the death of the Apepa, its wicked heart will be eaten, and its spiritual essence will be lost forever.

The Sacred Order of the Kush

When the true meaning of the Ma'at is known to you, it will mark your emergence into selflessness. The Ma'at is your historical road-map as we explore the remarkable world of the Kush. With the assistance of the Ma'at, this elder will show you the exact pathway to unity, creativity, honor, happiness, and peace. We call this path the way of the Kush.

The Beginning - Let there be Kush!

When the first point of the star Aries lay just left of the Vernal Equinox, the supreme God Amun descended upon the black volcanic earth. Amun stood upon the stone crust and surveyed that which he had created. He waived his left-hand over the molten sphere and the oceans of the world sprang-forth from the fiery stone. As the world cooled, with his right hand, Amun caused the earth to tremble as the Kushite motherland rose from the primordial sea. Amun named this land Alkebulan (African Eden), which is the original name for the African continent.

As the heavens blushed blue, the sky cleared, and the clouds moved in harmony with the winds. Trees, plants, and all the beast of the earth great and small, sprang-forth and spread themselves peacefully into the rivers and valleys of the earth. Fish filled the oceans, birds filled the sky, and the insects toiled as the entire world began to flourish.

Sensing that the world needed more, Amun reached for a small volcanic stone that had broken away from the base upon which he stood. He raised the stone to his mouth and spoke these words. "I will create a being in my image, and I will call him Shu, the first among men." Amun pressed the stone to his lips, and into it, he blew the essence of life. The stone transformed into a living man, and Amun rejoiced in his creation.

Shu the first male human being

Amun extended the index finger of his right hand and touched the forehead of the (human being) Shu. In that instance, that which was an empty shell became human. The Anu Shu had been given the gift of enlightenment and the ability to see himself.

Amun placed Shu upon the land and allowed him to roam. He immediately noticed that unlike all other living things, Shu was melancholy, directionless, and without purpose. He looked into the heart of man and learned of his need to be relevant. Seeing Shu as a less than perfect first attempt, Amun returned to his work.

The God of creation reached for another volcanic stone, and with it, he created the form that is a woman. "I will name her Tefnut," said Amun. He looked into the heart of Tefnut and found that she possessed harmony and vision beyond herself. The nature of Tefnut much pleased Amun, who declared that she should rule the earth, and Shu will protect her reign.

As Amun sat admiring his works, Bastet, the Goddess of motherhood, appeared before him. She removed the woman from the grasp of Amun, and by touching her, bestowed the ultimate power to create life. Amun was delighted and felt that the Goddess Bastet had greatly improved upon his work.

Through Tefnut, humanity was given a miraculous power previously reserved for the Gods. Humankind, in the form of a woman, was now capable of creating life, associating, and imagining things beyond space and time. The Anu named this divine gift, life, or the God Phase.

Tefnut the first female human being

Seeing the miraculous creation held by the Goddess Bastet, the God Thoth appeared before them. Thoth gently placed his staff upon the heads of the Anu, imparting to them the gift of wisdom and intelligence. Ptah, the God of skills, then appeared and gave humankind the gift of art and craftsmanship.

The Falcon God Horus appeared and bestowed unto humanity the moral pride of their accomplishments. Osiris gave the Anu the gift of the transcender, assuring that the ethical way of the Anu would never die. Isis gave humanity a righteous path to the afterlife. She also promised to protect the soul of the Anu as he/she traveled the final pathway in death.

Then the God Apedemak appeared. Apedemak, the Kushite lion God of War, bestowed unto humanity the gift of courage, athletic skill, and a desperate need for independence. As a result of these gifts, a Anu can never be dominated. The gift of independence made it impossible for any moral human being to be permanently enslaved, while the immoral can be enslaved by gold.

The God Bes wanted to lighten the heart of humanity, so he bestowed upon humankind the mathematics and euphoria of music and dance.

Seeing what the other Gods were up to, the mighty God Seth appeared. Seth is the God of Chaos and a rival for the thrown of Amun. He saw the creation of man as an opportunity to discredit Amun as the senior God.

Chaos believed that he should have been chosen supreme among the gods and would do anything to make this so. To prove his worthiness to be chief among the Gods, Chaos would use humanity to prove the incompetence of Amun.

Seth or Chaos the God of Evil

"I have a gift to bestow upon mankind," said Chaos. "I will give them the physical law of Chaos. No matter what the human does, all things in their universe will flow to disorder." The gift Chaos given to mankind was, in fact, a curse, and all of the other gods knew it. Chaos had effectively set humanity on a path of destruction even before he had officially begun. Humanity, in its infancy, had become the primary pawn in a war of the Gods.

When Harmony Entered the Room

To humanity's good fortune, there was one God left who had not contributed to the creation of humanity, and that was the Goddess Ma 'at. She is the Goddess of harmony, balance, and justice. Ma 'at is known as the quiet Goddess who appears as a petite black woman wearing a long flowing green dress adorned with emeralds. While the other Gods wore impressive crowns of gold and jewels, the Ma 'at wore a simple gold ribbon topped by an ostrich feather in her hair. Among the Anu, the feather is the ultimate symbol of justice!

The Goddess Ma 'at

Striking in her beauty and poise in her manner, the Goddess Ma 'at can appear in several forms. She can appear as an elder Anu female offering wisdom or as a young Anu maiden with a warning of impending doom. She speaks quietly and skillfully executes her strategies.

When the goddess Ma 'at appeared before Amun, she took no immediate action on humanity. Not wanting to offend the other Gods, the Ma 'at instead expressed concern to the Gods that they may be creating a being that is dangerous to itself.

"By providing your gracious gifts to mankind," said Ma' at, "you are allowing your creation to walk in the realm of the Gods with no knowledge of their true character or maturity."

Ma 'at's proclamation surprised Chaos because the two had always been on opposite sides of an issue. Chaos believed that the Ma 'at was supporting his position that Amun had errored in judgment.

Amun spoke directly to the Ma'at saying, "What would you have us do? The gifts have already been given." The Goddess Ma'at stepped forward and said, "with your blessing, I will train the Anu to adhere to a code of ethics. I will provide the Anu with a moral doctrine that will enable them to resist self-destruction. However, I would also ask a single favor of the great God Amun.

"Speak Ma'at," said Amun. "What favor would you ask?"

"The favor," said Ma'at "is that you designate my gift as the last to be given to humanity. I would like to see if the great creation of Amun can grow in virtue without future assistance from the Gods."

At that moment, the lion God of War Apedemak stepped forward to address Amun.

"I am Apedemak, the God of all warriors. I and I alone should be the trainer of the Anu warrior."

The Ma'at in a single motion, pointed her staff in the direction of Apedemak and said, "you have already given humanity courage, athletics and a fierce need for independence. You Apedemak, the great God of war, have given enough. I will train the warrior to have virtue because a warrior without virtue is little more than a rampaging thug." The other Gods gestured in agreement.

The God Amun said to Ma'at. "Give your gifts to mankind, and I will grant your request." Chaos was pleased with Amun's decision. He did not believe that any doctrine of decency could save humankind from the devastating effects of inevitable chaos.

Pleased with his final creation, the Lord God Amun stood before the universe and, in a thunderous voice, declared, "I am the supreme God Amun, creator of the Anu. There will be none greater upon this earth. The fate of the Anu and their ancestors is linked to the fate of the world upon which I have given them dominion."

The Curse of Enlightenment

The Anu-Kushites believed that enlightenment was a state of mental presence that enables you to pursue knowledge within the universe. Understanding is neither good nor bad but a force of nature that can ripple through the fabric of time, creating many alternative outcomes.

Enlightenment is also a lethal weapon with a doubled edge. One side of the blade generates the uniqueness of thought (creativity) that can lead to enormous personal and collective progress. The opposite side of the enlightenment blade promotes self-love, self-interest, and insatiable greed. The Anu must understand that when self is made the primary focus of the individual, he/she will leave a legacy of pain and disharmony.

The Kushites refer to the battle between self-interest versus the interest of the village, as the curse of enlightenment. A repeated mockery of the Anu among the Gods is that once humanity sees itself, it may never love another. This derision of humankind was a warning that the loss of kinship (brotherhood) will lead humanity into the arms of Chaos.

Chapter 2: The Myth of the Transcender

Harmony is the Essence of the Ma 'at

The Transcender is a mythical warrior trained in the tenets of the Ma 'at. This warrior also holds within its spirit the collective memories of the Kushite people. The essence of this warrior is allowed to transcend time and enter the consciousness of a worthy descendant. Their purpose is to protect against the extinction of the Ma 'at and the history of the Anu. Kutmet and Makasa were the first Kushites to be given the gift of transcendence. They were given this gift because each possessed an unusually pure heart.

Amun tested the purity of the first Transcenders by asking a single question. What is the name of the God of the Golden Gene? The answer of which is only known by the Gods and those who practice the way of the Kush. Amun decreed that when the Ma 'at ceases to exist, so will humanity.

The Kushites understood that there was a high probability that their society would fragment over time. They realized that any cycle of conflict could generate added divisions within the community. The Kush also understood that with each new social division, there was an increased chance for more conflict resulting in even more division.

Humankind is driven to divide itself while desperately needing to unite for collective survival. As you'll see within the history of the Kush, humanity is a creature susceptible to all sorts of divisiveness, each one a challenge to social harmony.

Two-hundred and forty-thousand of years after the enlightenment, the Anu prospered in the garden of Alkebulan, the African motherland. As their population grew, the elders noticed an increasing number of personal disputes. These social pressures were just as the Ma 'at had predicted.

One day, a conflict resulted in the death of a young Anu. So unusual was murder among the Kush that this tragedy triggered high alarm throughout the kingdom. The King and the elders asked the high priest to invoke the guidance of the Gods.

The Gathering of the Elders

In response to the first murder among the Anu-Kush, the most influential members of the community gathered in the forum. Kaa, the high priest of the Temple of Amun, stepped forward to speak to the gathering. Kaa declared, "I have consulted the Ma 'at and have concluded that Chaos is sowing disunity among our people. To protect the Kush from this threat, the Goddess Ma 'at has instructed us to build a new stone temple at Aswan. It will be called the Temple-of-Time."

Kaa decreed that the temple will contain a shield-shaped alter surrounded by a ring of lava from the fires of Jebel Marra. This sacred temple will be used to hold the souls of the transcenders who will carry the essence of the Kushite people throughout time.

Kaa explained, "within the Time-Temple upon their death, will be placed two Kushites chosen from among our finest warriors. The chosen must be one male and one female. The chosen must past Amun's purity test in order that their souls may transcend.

The Legend of Kushka and Kushkara

While it was not unusual for a female to represent her village, it was unprecedented for someone as young as Kushkara to be invited to the circle of elders. This accident of fate occurred because Kushkara's mother, the Candice, Kawimalo, had injured herself while riding her horse. The title of (Kanteki) pronounced Candice, was bestowed upon all high-ranking females of the Kush. The Candice Kawimalo was the governess of the village of Nuri and bore three daughters and no sons.

Candice Kawimalo decided to send her youngest daughter Kushkara to the upcoming Time-Temple ceremony in her place. Candice Kawi's two oldest daughters were with-child and unable to travel. It is said that Candice Kawi's fateful decision that day added two thousand years to the history of the Kush.

Several weeks before the Time-Temple ceremony, Kushkara and her sisters decided to shop for the fabric to create a new gown for the festival. While shopping in the village, the three came upon a kind fabric merchant. The two elder sisters occupied the time of the merchant, while Kushkara wondered the open-air shop. Kushkara came upon a young man who was clumsily folding fabrics.

"I'm Kushkara," she said as she warmly greeted the boy. I'm Kushka, he replied, as their eyes shyly met.

"Are you looking for something special?", begged Kushka in a friendly tone.

Kushkara smiled and gestured her interest in a blue cloth he was holding. She pretended to carefully examine the fabric within Kushka's arms as she spoke. "I like this blue one. This fabric will make a wonderful garment for the Time-Temple ceremony."

"You're going to the Transcender ceremony?" Said Kushka with a hint of surprise in his voice. "My instructor and I will also be there. My instructor wants to sell fabric at the ceremony. I don't think he cares for ritual, but he knows many potential customers will attend."

"Your instructor?" Asked Kushkara.

Kushka explained that he is an apprentice learning to buy

and sell fabrics. "I'm not very good at it," he confessed.

Kushka paused for a moment, then dared to express his real ambition with Kushkara.

"My real interest is to become an intellectual Ta-Sety," said Kushka.

"What is that?" said Kushkara as she strategically turned her face away from him to hide her amusement.

"An intellectual Ta-Sety is a warrior who creates battle strategies to protect the Kush," said Kushka, as he unconsciously inflated his chest with air.

"But wouldn't you need to be in the military to perform those duties?" said Kushkara in a joking tone.

Kushka smiled and gestured that he had flat feet as both erupted into laughter.

It was the bond of laughter that forged their friendship.

Kushkara sensed that her question had elicited a little discomfort in Kushka over his apparent social status. She never mentioned to him that she would be representing her entire village at the ceremony.

Kushka did feel a little embarrassed at his feeble attempt to elevate his perceived potential, but not at all insulted by her reserved but gleeful response. Kushka was too wise a young soul to allow mere words to blind him to the incredible beauty that was the beating heart of Kushkara.

The couple played every game possible to stay close to one another and talk. Kushkara would complain of the limited selection of fabric, while Kushka claimed the materials were of the highest quality. As their conversation turned flirtatious, Kushkara noted her sisters gesturing to her in the distance.

"I believe it is time for me to go," said Kushkara with reluctance in her voice. "I have yet to pick a piece of fabric. I think I'll take the blue one you were holding."

"May I bundle this fabric for you?" Said Kushka, attempting to hide his disappointment at their pending separation.

"You may," answered Kushkara as both walked to the front area of the open shop to complete the transaction. As the sisters left the merchant's shop, Kushkara looked over her shoulder for a parting peak at Kushka. Not at all surprised, she noted him watching her, each giving the other a gesture of a warm good-bye.

"Hope to see you at the ceremony," shouted Kushka, receiving only a glance and a smile from Kushkara, as the three sisters began their journey home.

The Time Temple Ceremony

The ceremony began at dusk as the elders entered the small pentagon-shaped forum, which was located a stone's throw from the newly constructed Time-temple. The Kushite elite began gathering inside the stone forum, choosing the appropriate seat that matched their tribe and status.

You could hear the voices of the people rhythmically mixed both inside and out of the forum halls. There were flicking torches that burned yellow gold against the temple interior while fading daylight filled every corner of the complex. The elders sat on step-like seats, elevated and facing inward to the center of the forum. A large colorful circular tile portrait of the God Amun marked the center of the forum and the place upon which the priest would make their choice.

Kushkara had already taken her mother's place among the elders as she sat attentively, watching the progress of the ceremony. Kushka and his merchant instructor had claimed a standing position inside the complex. Both were leaning shoulder to wall, looking inward as the ceremony proceeded.

Kushka found a vantage point where he could watch the service while simultaneously admiring the beauty of

Kushkara seductively wrapped in her powder blue gown, accented in gold ribbon. He was both surprised and distressed by her apparent status among the other more mature tribal leaders.

A hurtful thought and a sad feeling entered Kushka's mind that spoke of the impossibility of possessing that which he wanted most. Kushka watched from the corner of his eye as Kushkara sat on the edge of the third stair seat in the forum. She could not see him. Others were milling around the edges of the conference as ceremonial participants made their proclamations.

The High Priest Kaa stepped to the center of the forum and stood directly under the Apedemak skylight. In a booming voice, Kaa declared, "We the Kush are being undermined by the demon God Chaos. His evil minions have convinced many to embrace love-of-self at the expense of the family Kush. These divisions threaten the order of our society and, if not stopped, will lead to our destruction."

The High Priest Kaa turned to face each block of elders as he spoke. He extended his left hand in the direction of a group of senior priest and his right hand, open and softly gesturing to the elders as he spoke. "We, the priest of the Temple of Amun, have asked the Gods for a merciful solution to this recent curse of Kushite disharmony."

"The God Amun has answered our prayers," said Kaa. "He has brought us ten of our most exceptional warrior candidates, chosen for their great contributions to our communities throughout the nation. On this night, two will be chosen as transcenders of the Kush upon their death."

As Kaa spoke, the ten candidates, five men, and five women walked to the center of the forum where Kaa stood. The candidates were proceeded by two heavily adorn children, one male and one female.

The children were carrying burning incense jars as an offering to the God Anubis, the God of death. It is the God Anubis who must grant the transcender the power to cheat death by request of the high priest of the temple.

The candidates were dressed in long white togas with gold-trimmed collars, and a brown leather tie belt around their waist.

As the evening matured, there was an unusual quiet in the air. The usual sounds of nature just outside the forum were strangely absent. Unnoticed by the participants, a subtle trimmer began beneath their feet, warning of an imminent geologic event. The darkening sky's filled with ominous flashes of lighting just as the high priest Kaa invoked the spirit of the god Anubis.

The winds grew more energetic, and the earth beneath the forum began to tremble. The shaking ground began emitting deafening noises mixed with the sounds of cracking stone and increasingly concerned voices.

The elders and others at the gathering were starting to disperse quickly. It was not until the ceiling of the forum began to buckle that the people within the conference started to panic. As the forum foundations trembled, the ancient gods of the Kush gathered in the sky circle to watch the coming carnage below. Priest, elders, and citizens of the Kush began running in all directions as the earth violently convulsed.

The stone walls and foundations of the forum were sound, but the ceiling could not withstand the vibrating forces. As the forum foundations slipped outward, the massive stone ceiling began to crumble and collapse.

Kushka could see that the two children in the center of the forum were frozen in fear and in great peril from the falling debris.

The priests and transcender candidates had already run for their lives, leaving the two children to fend for themselves. Kushka rushed toward the children, and out of the corner of his eye could see Kushkara heading in the same direction.

Kushka and Kushkara came together and kneeled in one another's arms forming a human tint over the two children, cradling them under their bodies as they tightly embraced one another. As the north wall of the forum gave way, the massive ceiling stones cracked and collapsed upon Kushka, Kushkara, and the children.

The high priest Kaa and several other priests rushed back to the forum to retrieve the children, witnessing the sacrifice of Kushka and Kushkara. The stones were quickly removed, revealing the couple bloodied and crushed in their kneeling embrace with the two children alive, tucked uninjured between them.

The high priest Kaa with tears flowing down his face, looked to the heavens and declared, "we have found our transcenders! Anubis and the Goddess Ma 'at will be very pleased with our choice."

As the Gods watched this event, their hearts were moved by the selfless sacrifice of the young couple. It was unanimously agreed among the Gods, that Kushka and Kushkara possessed the golden gene and were granted the rank of Kushite transcender.

The burial of Kushka and Kushkara was held within the newly constructed time-temple, which was undamaged in the earthquake. Within the Temple, two crypts were placed, one on each side of a burning alter. Within the vaults were placed the remains of Kushka and Kushkara. Their souls on a deliberate journey in time in search of a worthy host.

The two children saved by the couple told the high priest Kaa that the last words whispered to them by Kushkara were these. "Fear nothing, for I will care for you!" These words were engraved on the crypt of Kushka and Kushkara, and the Temple was sealed for all eternity.

Chapter 3: The Historical Kushite (Part 1)

Were the Kushites Black African?

The Kushites were the children of the Anu, a black civilization that entered the Nile valley thousands of years before the creation of the Kemet (Egypt). I'm convinced that the Anu-Kushite was never in any real danger of disappearing from the historical record of humankind. Why? Because someone was bound to ask the question, who were they?

Forty-six years ago, I asked my university professor of ancient history, who was the origin of Egypt? This fundamental question perplexed my instructor and led me directly to the Anu-Kush. When the who, what, and why questions are forced upon our arrogant academics, histories long ignored by western institutions are joyously rediscovered.

Kushites Speak from the Grave

The Kushites did not want to be forgotten! To assure that they were not forgotten, the Kushites built thousands of temples, monuments, and tombs all over Egypt and Sudan. The Kush also documented their legacy in the graves of their royal dead.

It appears that the Kushite myth of the transcender is also fulfilling its purpose. The soul of the transcender patiently waits to be reborn in the bodies of the righteous human being. Its purpose is to reignite the way of the Kush and bring to fruition the universal Kushite code of human decency.

The transcenders of today are aggressively reintroducing Kushite history and the tenets of the Ma'at to the world. As the tomb of Kushka and Kushkara were sealed, the mystic Kushite came to an end, and the historic Kushite emerged.

The Relevance of Kushite History

Every Kushite (moral human being) of African ancestry, must learn his/her history in order to feel complete. I'm not just referring to the recent past, but also deep history. Deep history takes us back thousands of years before any of the modern religions or ideologies existed. Deep history also enables us to see the African connection to the formation of the modern world.

This historical connection is called cultural continuity. Without knowing your history, you cannot develop a proper sense of self-possession. Without an appreciation of self-possession, you risk being unfairly defined by others. Worst yet, you risk the damaging psychological effects of unconsciously accepting someone else's biased definition of who you are.

> If you are unable to accept the Kush, you will be equally incapable of accepting yourself.

Understand that the concept of self-possession demands that you define yourself. Do not allow others to tell your stories, especially your history. Once you've experienced and accept the Kushite perspective of history as I have, you will come to appreciate the full extent of your historical importance to the entire world.

Who is the Anu (Black African)?

As a person of African ancestry and as a biologist, the answer to this question is easy. The black African is everything that is humanity. Black Africans, also known as the Anu, are the origin of humanity, race, culture, civilization, and the written word. Does my pronouncement appear to be too large of a historical bite? Then hold on to your seat! This text is a short introduction to Anu-Kushite history that may change your mind.

Modern historians are just beginning to push back the cloak of ignorance that has hidden the incredible history of the African continent and its people. When we examine the African in all of its diversity, we find many contradictions to the modern view of the development of humankind, language, and civilization.

When modern science began turning its attention to the little-known culture of the Kushite, they discovered a genuine historical enigma. The generally accepted historical view of the Kushite is that they were black African people who lived quietly along the southern Nile. Although the Kush existed for thousands of years, the western opinion was that they did so as a collection of struggling backwater cultures. Many Eurocentric text about African history contain unsubstantiated comments cynically suggesting an inferiority of black culture. These culturally biased opinions are not just hurtful; they are also totally incorrect.

The most common insult of the Kush is the western insistence that the Kush were subordinate to the Egyptians. You'll often see this unproven assertion written in Egyptian historical manuals. Except for a few politically motivated wall carvings and stelas, there is little in the historical records that would support Egyptian dominance of the Kushite. Much of what I've discovered about the Kush leads me to believe that just the opposite may have been true.

There is significant circumstantial evidence that the Egyptians were both subordinate and dependent upon the Kush. Keep in mind that dominance is a western cultural anomaly having no real relevance to ethnic history. The Kush believed that dominance was a violent tool used by those lacking the moral or intellectual ability to lead. My personal belief is that the two cultures were in-fact mutually dependent and remarkably similar in both customs and beliefs. I also suspect that both the Kemet (Egyptian) and the Kushite had the same Anu origin.

Where the Nubians Kushites?

The short answer to this question in a foreign since is yes, Nubians were Kushites. However, a more accurate name for the Nubian would be the term Anu. The Anu or Amelineau are the prehistoric black people who were the first to inhabit the lands that became Kemet and Kush. If this statement is true, then the original Egyptians were also Nubians or Anu. When you prob deeper into ethnic Kushite (Anu) history, you quickly encounter a variety of names used by foreigners to describe the indigenous people of Africa.

The most common terms used by foreigners to describe Africans of the north-east were Egyptian, Nubian or Ethiopian. These terms were of Greek origin and did not define a specific tribe. These terms were used by foreigners as a generalization to describe the various black African people.

The ancient people of this region never referred to themselves as Egyptian or Nubian. Egyptian means black, Nubian means (Gold), and Ethiopian is a Greek word meaning (dark or burnt face). While the term Ethiopian is used by one modern predecessor of the Kemet/Kush today, the name Nubian is not. The word Nubian is a term used by westerners to obscure the identity of the African people known as the Kushite (moral human being). Using foreign terms to describe one's self is a self-destructive approach that can lead to the loss or distortion of your history!

The Kushites referred to themselves as the Anu-Kush or Kushites. The Kush also called themselves the Meroitic, Dongolan, Ta-Sety (people of the bow), the forever-men, and the Kerma people. All of these terms used to describe the Anu-Kushite have a self-defining historical foundation while the term Nubian does not.

Had the term Kushite been used by historians instead of Nubian, perhaps the Kush would have been harder to disregard as an irrelevant culture. I bring this naming issue to your attention because it is a key reason why Kushite history has remained obscured for so long. After fifty years of Kushite study, I can assure you that the Kush would never refer to themselves as Nubians. Frankly, I believe they would have found the term Nubian insulting. Out of respect for our ancestors, we will refer to them as they would refer themselves, The Kush!

The Power of the Word Kushite

This elder has been speaking to others about the Kush for nearly fifty years. It was during several of these conversations that I noted the incredible power inherent in claiming myself to be Kush. While I am not a direct descendent of the Kush, it is part of my rich cultural heritage as a member of the Africa diaspora. The term Kushite has a far deeper meaning to the educated colonialist than you might imagine. When you declare yourself a Kushite in the presence of an informed colonialist, you are declaring your unapologetic understanding of self. This declaration can be intimidating to the colonialist even if the person is not at all racist. However, to the educated racist, the word Kushite is devastating.

The word Kushite reminds the racist of who is the biological and cultural child and who is the parent. The term Kushite places the racist in a subordinate position before he/she can open their misinformed mouth. In so many ways, the word Kushite is a representation of the modern dynamic between black and white. One wants to culturally dominate, while the Kushite wants to culturally consume.

The term Kushite takes the colonial mind back to a remote and unfamiliar time in human history, a place he/she is not at all comfortable. The historical period before 3000 B.C. is utterly off-limits to many western cultures. This historical discomfort is especially true when you add a religious component. Deep time leaves westerners culturally alienated from the rest of humanity. Fortunately, their salvation also lay in the tenets of the Ma'at.

Chapter 4: The Historical Kushite (Part 2)

What Makes the Kushites Unique?

The Kushites are the oldest of the known black African civilizations that were both a nation and an empire. If it were not for the Kush, interior Africa would have been overrun by numerous parasitic cultures in antiquity. The Kushites are uniquely responsible via their military prowess, for the preservation of African lands and African cultural heritage.

The incredibly ancient Kushites were a proud and complicated people. Like many African cultures today, the Kushites had a tradition of using oral, hieroglyphic, written, and transcendent (afterlife) methods of preserving their history. Their verbal and symbolic traditions were an extraordinarily powerful method of retaining cultural cohesiveness.

The priests and elders of the Kush specialized in these oral traditions and were capable of recalling story's thousands of years old. To this very day in Sudan, there are still a handful of these oral historians remaining.

The Kushites controlled a vast territory that ranged from the origin of the Nile in Ethiopia to the Nile delta. At its peak, Kushites controlled a regional area encompassing Egypt, Ethiopia, the

Levant, Sudan and beyond. The Kush referred to this ancient collective as the Kingdom of the Two Cobras.

There is historical evidence that in Neolithic times the Kushites may have controlled territories from modern-day Uganda to Persia and beyond. The ethnic Kushites existed long before there was an Egyptian nation. The Anu-Kush claimed to be the origin of the Egyptian culture and religion. The Kush have also, in the distant past, declared their historic right to rule Kemet (Egypt).

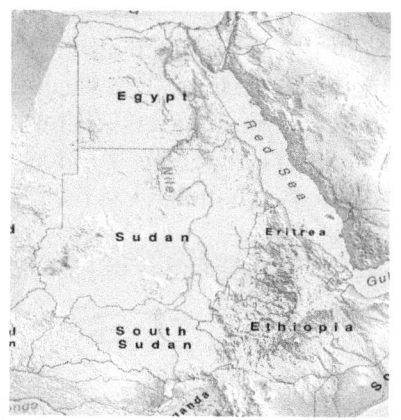

Original Kushite Kingdom of the Two Cobras

There are so many similarities between the Egyptians and the Kushites that it would be impossible to deny the unique relationship between the two. There is no doubt that each had an incredible influence on the other. While it appears that the Egyptians contributed to the Kushite culture, it is not clear how much impact the Kushites had on the ancient Egyptians. This text will change that dynamic!

The reason for this discrepancy is simple. The Egyptian culture has enjoyed widespread attention by the outside world while the Kushite remained almost entirely unknown.

I believe that you cannot accurately tell the history of Egypt without including its origin, the Anu-Kush. We also cannot determine the complexity or extent of the Kushite contribution to civilization without the dedicated science of Kushology (the study of the Kush). Once the science of Kushology is created, we can begin to place the long-needed focus required to decipher the

Kushite language and extract their many incredible secrets.

The Kushite View of the World

It's essential to understand how Kushites saw themselves with respect to other peoples and nations. In regard to people, the Kushites believed that they were the origin of humanity, the father and mother of the human race. They felt that all other people were the children of the Kush, who had merely begun a new village in another location. This parental attitude was especially apparent when it came to the Kemet. The Kushites believed that there was a tribal, linguistic, religious, and cultural bond between themselves and the Egyptians. The Kush also believed that the separation of the two nations was the result of the curse of Chaos.

The Curse of Chaos

The Beast that eats itself

In time a family will become a village, a village will become a tribe, a tribe will become a state, and a state will become a rival.

Early Kushites saw no difference between themselves and the Kemet. Both tribes in the mind of the Kush had the same Anu origin. The Kushites believed that what was born of the Kush was Kush. This kinship did have one crucial caveat. A genuine child of the Kush had to learn and accept the essential tenets of the Ma'at (code of human decency).

The Early Kushites

The Anu-Kushites, like most other civilizations, began modestly. Their population was primarily agrarian. As the Anu-Kushite culture developed, there is ample evidence that their communities migrated from small villages to medium-sized cities. These growing cities flourished through trade in cattle, horses, crafts, manufacturing, and the processing of natural resources. The Kushites were kings, nobles, merchants, farmers, fishermen, traders, artisans, priests, government workers, and all manner of the military.

As their civilization grow, the Kush became successful merchants dealing in raw and finished goods. There is ample evidence that Kushite commercial trade covered much of the then known world. Artifacts found in homes and burials throughout the Kushite kingdom contained jewelry, weapons, pottery, etc., from distant and remote lands. While much of the Kushite trade was with Kemet and other African nations, there is also evidence of significant business in the Levant and areas much further east.

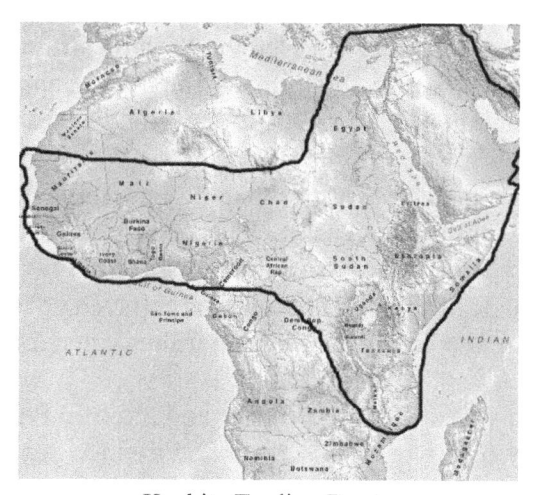

Kushite Trading Routes

The Kush also made a tremendous amount of trade with central and southern African nations. These trade routes would have taken the Kushites into Kenya, Great Zimbabwe, the Congo, and beyond. This view of the Kushite reveals a thriving trade-based civilization known from the near east to the western coast of

Alkebulan (Africa).

Kushite Government

The Kushites appear to have had a complex centralized government with a monarchical structure headed by a King, Queen or Pharaoh. They also appear to have been a matriarchal society with many women in positions of power. Similar to the Egyptians, the Kushite rulers believed that they ruled by divine right. However, the Kushite Kings were not an all-powerful god-like entity like that of the Egyptian Pharaoh. The Kushite Kings shared power with governmental officials, priests, chiefs, and elders. In short, the Kushite system appears to have been a bit less autocratic when compared to the Kemet.

Although rule within a family line was common, Kushites did not necessarily acquire kingship by inheritance. The Kush preferred the best leadership as defined by the Ma'at rather than strict biological inheritance. For instance, there is a historical reference to the rise of the Pharaoh Taharqa. This Kushite leader was a military commander who led the Kushite army in many battles before ascending to the throne. Taharqa ascended to the throne of Egypt and the Kush in 690 BC and ruled for twenty-six years.

There is a historical rumor that the Pharaoh Taharqa was not the son of the previous Kushite Pharaoh Shebitku. Taharqa may not have even been a significant member of the royal family. It is believed Taharqa was chosen Pharaoh by a coalition of the priest of Amun, the chiefs, elders, and military generals.

Taharqa was a Kushite Warrior and the fifth Pharaoh of the 25th Dynasty of Egypt. He is also known as the Savior of Jerusalem and one of the greatest builders in Egyptian history. Taharqa was the supreme ruler of both Egypt and the Kushite Kingdom, and he proudly wore the crown of the two cobras, a title achieved only by the Kushite Pharaohs.

The Kushite Priesthood

Like Kemet, the Kushites had a powerful class of temple priests. The priests were in charge of the spiritual and ceremonial aspects of the domain. The primary duties of the priest included advising the King, public rituals, spiritual guidance, burial ceremonies, caring for the temples, and communicating with the gods. The priests were also power brokers among the Kush and, like most religious institutions, competed for tax-free wealth and influence.

Kings of the Kush

The known Kushite kings begin around 1900 B.C. This means that there may be more than 3000 years of Kushite rulers that remain unknown to us. Hopefully, this will change with exploration and research. The Kushite Kings listed below are divided into five time periods. Each period contains the known rulers. Please note that there were a significant number of female rulers among the Kush. These female rulers were often given the royal designation of Queen, Queen-mother, and Kandeke, pronounced (Candice).

Kings of the Kermatic Period:

King Kaa -1900 BCE

King Teriahi-1880 BCE

King Awawa - 1870 BCE

King Utatrerses – 1850 BCE

King Nedjeh 1550 BCE

Kandeke Makeda -1005 - 950 BCE

King Aserkamani – 950 BCE

King Seb – 930 BCE

Candice Kadimalo – 920 BCE

Kushite Kings of Napata Period:

King Alara – 795 – 752 BC

King Kashta – 765 – 752 BC

Kushite Pharaohs Egyptian Period:

Pharaoh Piankhi - 752 - 721 BC

Pharaoh Shabaka – 721 – 706 BC

Pharaoh Shebitku - 706 – 690 BC

Pharaoh Taharqa. - 690 - 664 BC

Pharaoh Tantamani – 664 – 654 BC

Kushite Kings Post Egypt

King Atlanersa – 654 – 642 BC

King Senkamanisken - 642 – 620 BC

Queen Anlamani – 620 – 600 BC

King Aspelta – 600 – 580 BC

King Aramatle-qo – 568 – 555 BC

King Malonaqen – 555 – 542 BC

King Anlamaye – 542 – 538 BC

King Amaninatakilebte – 538 – 519 BC

King Karkamani – 519 – 510 BC

King Amaniastabarqa – 510 – 487 BC

King Siaspiqa – 487 – 468 BC

King Nasakhma – 468 – 463 BC

Candice King Malewiebamani – 463 – 435 BC

Candice King Talakhamanie – 435 – 431 BC

King Amanineteyerike – 431 – 405 BC

King Baskakeren – 405 – 390 BC

King Harsiotef – 369 – 350 BC

King Akhraten – 350 – 335 BC

King Nastasen – 335 – 315 BC

King Amanibakhi – 3nd Century BC

King Aktisanes - 3nd Century BC

King Aryamani - 3rd Century BC

King Kash (Kush) - 3rd Century BC

King Piankhi II - 3rd Century BC

Candice King Sabrakamani 2nd Century BC

King Arakamani (Arkamaniqo) - 270 - 260 BC

King Amanislo – 260 – 250 BC

King Amantekha - 2nd Century BC

King Sheshep – 2nd Century BC

King Arnekhamani - 2nd Century BC

King Arqamani - 2nd Century BC

King Adikhalami - 2nd Century BC

Queen Shanakdakhete - 2nd BC

Queen Tanyidamani - 1st Century BC

King Naqyrinsan - 1st Century BC

Queen Aqrakamani – 29 - 25 BC

King Teriteqas - 25 - 20 BC

Kandeke Amanirenas - 1st Century AD

Kandeke Amanishakheto - 1st AD

Kandeke Nawidemak - 1st AD

King Amanikhabale – 1st AD

King Natakamani – 1st AD

Queen Amanitore – 1st AD

King Shorkaror - 1st AD

King Pisalar – 2nd AC

King Amanitaraqide – 2nd AC

King Amanitenmemide - 2nd AC

Kandeke Amanikhatashan - 2nd AC

King Teritnide – 2nd AC

Kandeke Teqerideamani I - 2nd AD

Kandeke Tamelerdeamani – 3nd AD

King Adeqatali – 3nd AD

Kandeke Takideamani -3rd AD

King Tarekeniwal- 3rd AD

King Amanikhalika - 4rd AD

King Aritenyesbokhe - 4rd AD

King Amanikhareqerem - 4rd AD

King Teritedakhatey - 4th AD

King Aryesbokhe - 5th AD

King Teqerideamani II - 5th AD

Kandeke Maleqorobar - 5th AD

King Yesbokheamani - 5th AD

Queen Lakhideamani – Late 5th - 6th AD

Kushite Royal Naming Convention

Kushite royal names were not always handed down within a royal family or used as a result of its popularity. Kushite names were almost always symbolic and sometimes exclusive. Kushite Kings were named as a result of a personality trait or an event related to the individual's life. The naming convention used by the Kushite Pharaohs reveals that the King had two names, one Kush and one Kemet. It was the King's prerogative to choose which name would be displayed on monuments.

Kushite Pharaohs used both Kushite and Kemet names in inscriptions. The Kemet (Egyptian) name might be used on a statue, while the King's Kushite name is used in everyday governess. The Kushite name appears to have been the family name, while the Kemet name was chosen as the King's public persona.

That Anu-Egyptians used a bi-cultural naming convention in the first place is fascinating. The Kemet and Kushites lived together for millennia. There's a high probability of widespread intercultural family integration that could explain the mixed-use of names. Occam's razor states that the simplest explanation is usually correct. In other words, the Egyptian and the Kush were either the same people or a standard breeding population resulting in a mixed culture. In either case, they were still both of Anu origin.

There are many secrets hidden in the names of the Kushite rulers. For instance, there is a very commonly used name-within-a-name called Amani, meaning (harmony, peace, or justice) used primarily by Kushite royalty. Interestingly, in old Swahili, Amani also means the protector of harmony, peace, and justice. Names in Kushite culture are also a hint to the philosophical or personality type of the ruler who chose the name.

The Kushite Female

The Kushite was one of the most progressive societies in the ancient world. The Kush believed that the female is the driving force of civilization and should preside over all things related to the governess, social norms, justice, and morality. This belief enabled Kushite females to exercise enormous power within society. The Kush believed that it is the female spirit of the Ma'at, not the volatile essence of the male god Apedemak, that should guide the hearts and minds of the people.

Kushite women wielded as much social and economic power as did the male. Kushite society elevated the female and provided the world with an impressive number of highly successful female rulers. Case in point is the famous female ruler referred to by the Kush as the Warrior Queen, Candice Amanirenas (Amani-Renas).

There are multiple historical references to powerful Kushite queens standing toe-to-toe in battles against Greek and Roman invaders. One of the best-known conflicts occurred in 24 BC, led by the Kushite Candice Amanirenas and her uncle or brother Prince Akinidad.

The Candice Amanirenas commanded the forces that destroyed an invading Roman army, forcing their withdrew from Kushite lands. The virtuous female Kushite Warrior was considered to be the earthly representation of the Goddess Ma 'at. Female Kushite rulers were also buried with the same majesty as that of the great Kushite Kings.

Kushite Society

The Kushites were an ancient and highly sophisticated society that originated from the heart of Sudan in East Africa. The historical place of Kushite origin is known today as the cradle of humanity.

While the climate has changed over the centuries, some parts of the Kushite homeland were known to be arid. Some areas of Sudan were a challenge for agriculture, which made the Nile a critical resource. While the Kush was not as dependent upon the Nile as the Kemet, both used it for the same purpose. The Nile was a source of wonder, protein, transportation, and agriculture.

Shaduf on the river Nile at the Ancient city of Kerma

In the north, the annual floods filled the Nile valley with fertile topsoil that enabled these ancient populations to survive. Both cultures built Shadufs along the riverbanks to extract water for drinking and bathing. The shaduf was also used to remove the water to irrigate crops during the dry season. The Kushites were also believed to have modified the shaduf into the world's earliest known cranes. These modified shadufs were believed to have been used in the construction of the narrow-based Kushite pyramids.

The artwork on the previous page depicts a common shaduf. These dipping buckets are still used in the rural areas of the Nile today. Fishing was also an essential part of Egyptian and Kushite lifestyle and occurred on both the Nile and the Red Sea. There are also larger boats depicted in Kushite and Egyptian artwork used for transportation, trade, and war.

Kushites were heavily involved in animal husbandry. While most animals were used for food and agriculture, the horse was revered by the Kush. The beloved horse was used for transportation, personal recreation, and war. There is a fascinating Kushite legion surrounding the horse. Historians believe that horses were introduced during the Hyksos invasion of Egypt. The Hyksos conquered the Kemet in approximately 1720 B.C.

However, there is archeological evidence that horses were being used in both Egypt and Sudan long before the Hyksos invaded. The Punt, another branch of the Kushite family, was known to trade horses and elephants in the region long before the Hyksos arrived. Regardless of how the horse was introduced, the Kushites took them to heart. Kushites revered the horse for their strength, power, and beauty. There is extensive evidence of Kushite domestication of horses throughout the kingdom.

Kushites considered horses to be sacred. It is rumored that the great Kushite Pharaoh Piankhi so cherished his warhorse, that he ordered it to be buried with him.

Chapter 5: The Historical Kushite (Part 3)

Where the Ancient Kemet Anu?

The author of this text believes (unapologetically and without hesitation) that the original Egyptians were black and the children of the Anu. The Anu is the prehistoric black African people that created all of the fundamental cultural components that we now consider Egyptian. Every piece of ancient evidence supports this racial fact and more. Not only were the first Egyptians black, but they were also the origin of what some call civilization.

The Kushite A-Group genetic hypothesis supports the migration into northern Egypt by the Kerma people (Kushites) as early as 8500 B.C. These findings support the existence of ethnic Anu from the Dongola region of southern Sudan to the Egyptian delta and beyond.

The migratory pattern mentioned above may explain why King Menes (Narmer), the first Pharaoh of Egypt, took no hostile action against the Anu-Kushites upon separation of the two kingdoms. Menes and the Kush were both Anu. This means that the original Egyptians were ethnically Anu just like the Kush. See the bust of Menes above.

Menes, the founder of Egypt and the first pharaoh, created his new nation above the first cataract of the Nile circa 3150 B.C. At this point in history, the area above the first cataract was inhabited by ethnic Anu. The Anu-Kemet would have easily been the majority ethnic population in this entire region at this time. Population dominance by the Anu-Kemet is supported by genetic studies and artifacts found within collective burials. The Lands south of the first cataract also remained ethnically Anu during this same period.

Shouts of an Anu-Kushite Origin

While migratory genetic patterns are a powerful tool, they are not definitive proof of the origin of Kemet. It could be that some other outside force invaded the area around the first cataract and formed a new nation in that location. This new nation could have absorbed a substantial population of ethnically Anu people.

Even if common graves contained identifiable Kushite corpses from this period, they would be scarce given the terrain at that time. Keep in mind that we are discussing events that occurred more than 6000 years ago. Artifacts found in these ancient graves do point to a common Anu origin, but this is not definitive evidence of provenance.

Case in point. If 5000 years from now, we happened upon a native American gravesite, would their corpses and artifacts lead us to believe that the native American was the origin of the United States? Probably not! We would need more evidence. However, it might lead us to believe that the Native American was the precursor of the people who created the United States, rather true or not.

We would also need to consider the graves of all those other folks we would find. The native graves would undoubtedly be older than that of the Europeans. But the grave type and burial practices would show different cultural norms. These varied cultural norms would lead us to consider migration or invasion. To determine the parentage of the U.S., we would need more evidence.

In my hypothetical search for the origin of the United States, we would also need to consider written history, cultural artifacts, cultural mythology, language, architecture, historical records, and geography. My point is this! Human genetics and migratory patterns alone cannot definitively reveal the origin of the U.S. any more than it can determine the origin of Egypt.

In my determination to prove the Anu-Kush as the origin of Egypt, I have expressed the following circumstantial evidence:

1. Our Egyptian origin timeframe is around 3150 BC.

2. Migratory patterns and genetic studies from the Egyptian region in 3150 BC point to a population that was primarily of black African origin. However, other bodies found in the future may have a genetic source outside the continent.

3. Mythology and artifacts lead us to believe that Egypt was created from conflict. The conflict appears to have been between people of the same racial origin (Anu).

4. After the epic battle for Egypt, the native population did not change in appearance or location. There was no evidence of post-conflict population migrate, deportation, or phenotypic change.

5. The bust of Menes is a strong archaeological hint of the ethnic background of the alleged first Pharaoh of Egypt. This artifact was discovered in the tomb of Menes at Abydos, Egypt. Menes appears to be phenotypically Anu. This would ethnically label Menes an Anu-Kemet.

When evaluating a history as remote as 3150 BC, mythology and historical facts can be challenging to separate. To continue my argument for the Anu origin of Egypt, I need to turn to the accepted beliefs of traditional Egyptologists. I will accomplish this by taking a closer look at Menes and his newly formed Kingdom of Egypt.

The Egyptian War of Independence

The Menes' conflict with the Anu-Kush is best described as a war of independence, or a civil war when considering the current level of evidence.

According to traditional Egyptologists, the pre-dynastic period in Egyptian ended circa 3150 BC, and the age of the Pharaoh kings began. King Menes, the so-called Scorpion King, is designated the first Pharaoh of Egypt.

At this point in history, the area that would become Kemet or Egypt, was comprised of several competing Anu-Kushite city-states. Before the formal creation of Egypt, Menes had to defeat the only people existing in this area at that time. That people were the Anu-Kush.

Logic forces me to consider that Menes's war was with the Anu-Kush. The Stela at Abydos called the Narmer Palette reinforces my belief. The palette shows several representations that would match that of the ethnic Anu.

The Reason for the War

The reason for the Menes war with the Anu-Kush is purely speculative. Why would Menes want to break away from the Anu? Why would any nation made up of the same people divide? Perhaps the Anu-Egyptian war of independence was based on greed or a distaste for moral Anu-Kushite leadership. Corruption of any type within an Anu- Kushite government would have been considered a direct attack upon harmony. Fraud among the Anu-Kush would not be tolerated, which may have led to war.

Perhaps the reason for the Anu-Egyptian war of independence was the need to control one's destiny. Humanity's insatiable desire to divide and become something different is a common characteristic of the human species. Whatever the reason for war, according to Narmer's palette, a conflict between Anu-Egyptians and the Anu-Kush did occur.

Another factor that leads me to believe that the Anu-Egyptian/Kushite conflict was a civil war is Menes's place of birth. Menes was reportedly born in the Thinite Nome area north of Luxor. The site of Menes's birth rules out a foreign invasion in the creation of Egypt.

After the Civil War

After the war with the Anu-Kush, the Anu-Kushites continued to control Aswan and the lands below the first cataract. This post-war control by the Anu-Kush leads me to believe that Menes did not defeat the Kushite nation. My theory is that Menes conquered a local authority (city-state governor) within the pre-Egyptian Anu-Kushite kingdom.

The main Anu-Kushite seat of power may have been located further south at Kerma, Napata, or even Meroe in Sudan. The above analysis of the Egyptian/Kushite conflict is more circumstantial evidence that the Anu-Egyptian was a child of the Anu-Kush.

The Written Language of the Anu-Egyptian

The ancient script of the Anu-Egyptian contains hidden clues that lead to a possible Anu origin of the language. The historical records indicate that the Egyptian language was known as the Mdju-netjer or Word of God. Anu-Egyptian mythology implies that this writing was given to the Egyptians by the God Thoth. The God Thoth was prominent among the earliest Anu-Kush.

More importantly, there is recent archeological evidence this same language existed before the birth of the Egyptian nation by at least two hundred years. If the Egyptian script did exist this early in history, this would suggest an Anu origin for the language of God.

The earliest known examples of hieroglyphic writing in the land that would become Egypt dates to approximately 3300 BC. This existence date implies that God's language existed before the birth of the Egyptian nation. If Menes were the first Pharaoh and already possessed this literature, this would mean that he inherited the language.

The circa 3300 BC inception date for the Egyptian script is comparable to the generally accepted creation of the first written language Cuneiform. The date, 3300 BC, suggests that Cuneiform may not be the earliest written language. Cuneiform is believed to have been created by a civilization called the Sumerians around 3200 BC. The Sumerians were located in the area near Babylon in Mesopotamia (Iraq) in the ancient city-state of Uruk.

It is important to note that Cuneiform is not in and of itself a language. It is a system of symbols that can be adapted to form a written version of a language.

Cuneiform symbols were used to create a written script for several unique cultures. Cuneiform enabled these cultures to formulate a written form of their language. Civilizations using Cuneiform included but were not limited to the Sumerians, Akkadian, Assyrian, and the Babylonian Empire.

Anu-Egyptian Script is not Related to Cuneiform

The ancient Egyptian language does not appear to be linguistically related to cuneiform. Early Egyptian hieroglyphic script is also believed to have been developed prior to 3200 B.C. This date leads one to wonder if Egyptian writing is not much older than cuneiform, making it the first written language on earth.

This 3200 B.C. date also reminds us of a related story about King Menes the Scorpion King. The archeologists are now theorizing that there existed a sophisticated people or nation before the time of Menes. Well duh! This pre-Egyptian civilization appeared to be very Egyptian in tradition, language, and culture.

While modern Egyptologists still refuse to believe that these earlier Egyptians were Anu, they are finally moving in this direction. The latest theory is that before there was an Egypt, there was another predynastic King. This preexisting king was designated as Scorpion One. Menes is now considered Scorpion King Two. These Kings were named Scorpion primarily because of a scorpion seal found in the burial of Menes.

Currently, we do not understand the relationship, if any, between Scorpion King one and two. There appears to be a significant time gap between the two Scorpion Kings of up to 100 years. This implies that there may have been many kings before Menes. If this one-hundred-year-old date is even close to being correct, this means that there was a dynastic line predating Egypt. This older group appears to be the cultural precursor to Egyptian civilization. The only related group existing in this area at this period of time were the Anu!

A Gradual Process

I would argue that great civilizations don't just suddenly burst into existence. Cultures develop over time and are usually related to those that came before them. Why would this not also be true of Egypt? The independence of Egypt appears to have been a gradual process. Scorpion King One was (maybe) the first of two Kings whose actions are believed to have eventually resulted in an independent Egyptian state. Perhaps, King Scorpion One was the inventor of the Egyptian national identity that would later drive the Egyptian war of independence from the Anu-Kush. The existence of Scorpion King One begs the question, were there Kings before him? According to the Anu-Kush, their Kings go back another two or three thousand years. I will discuss the evidence supporting the existence of these pre-Egyptian Kings later in this text.

King Scorpion II (Menes)

King Scorpion II is the more famous (Dynasty One) leader who would become Egypt's first pharaoh. Scorpion II is believed to be the Pharaoh Menes, also known by his Kushite name Narmer. The Pharaoh Menes is given credit for the creation of the formal Egyptian state around 3150 B.C. The history of Menes comes from a palette found shortly after the discovery of his tomb. This stone document was named the Narmer Palette.

The Narmer Palette is believed to depict Egypt's great battle of independence that established the Egyptian state. King Menes's great victory that resulted in the creation of Egypt is commemorated on the Narmer Palette, shown below. However, the Narmer Palette is puzzling to me on several levels.

Narmer Palette

After Menes's military victory, the new King Menes is not depicted wearing the combined crown of upper and lower Egypt. The white crown represents lower Egypt and the red crown, upper Egypt. A combined crown would indicate that Menes ruled a united nation. On the palette, Menes wears only the crown of lower Egypt, which was the land above the first cataract. If Menes had defeated the Kushite nation, I would expect him to be depicted wearing the double crown.

Please note that both crowns are depicted on the Narmer Palette. The two crowns imply that the concept of an upper and lower Egypt existed before Egypt's war of independence. How could there have been an upper and lower Egypt before there was an Egypt? This finding would only make sense if prior to the war of independence, Kemet and Kush were one.

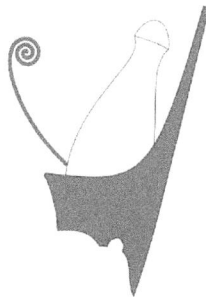

Double crown of the Egyptian/Kushite Pharaoh

On the front side of Narmer palette, Menes is shown holding a prisoner by the hair with the intent to execute. This picture demonstrates Menes dominance over the defeated enemy. On the backside of the Narmer palette, please note the defeated King in the upper left-hand corner. This King is wearing the crown of Upper Egypt.

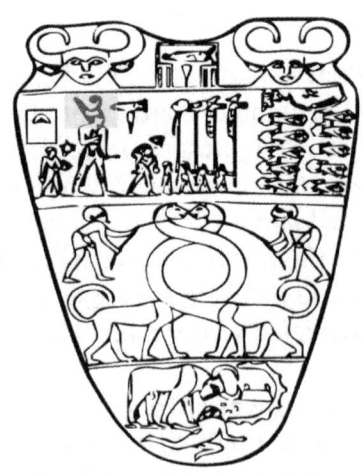

Backside of Narmer's Pallet

The conventional definition of upper and lower Egypt makes no sense because Egypt had just sprung into existence. The obvious flaw in the traditional theory is that at the time of Menes, there was no Egypt. The nation of Egypt had yet to be created. But there could have been an upper and lower Kush. Also, if Menes had conquered the entire Kushite nation, both upper and lower, why is he not wearing the double crown representing this victory?

This palette leads me to believe that Menes defeated a northern province of the Anu-Kush, aka (lower Egypt). The Egyptian interpretation of the back of the Narmer palette would read as follows:

"A great force of the King of Upper Egypt (Anu-Kushite) confronted Menes in preparation for battle. The land of the two cobras stood eye to eye equal in the eyes of God. A great battle ensued, and with the help and blessing of the God Hapi the bull, the Anu-Kushite army was set into flight."

I believe that Egyptology has misinterpreted the concept of upper and lower Egypt. The modern view of upper and lower Egypt is defined as northern Egypt (delta region) and southern Egypt (Memphis to Aswan). I believe that the above definition of upper and lower Egypt did not exist at the time of Menes. The current description of upper/lower

Egypt came later in history. So what was the original meaning of the term upper and lower Egypt?

Kushite symbol of the two Cobras

When I first saw the wall sculpture above representing the two cobras, I immediately knew what this meant. This sculpture is proof of my theory of an upper and lower Anu-Kushite civilization that predates Egypt. A land that existed prior to Menes! The Kushites referred to upper and lower Kush as the land of the two cobras. To the Anu-Kush, the area above Aswan was lower Kush. The area from Aswan to the Dongola region was considered upper Kush. The above interpretation implies, according to the Kush, that Kemet and Kush are two parts of the same nation held together by the Kushite war god Apedemak shown between them.

Menes Relationship to Egyptian Script

King Menes is linked to Egyptian writing because many small ivory transaction tags with pictorial hieroglyphs were found in his tomb at Abydos. These symbols imply that the first Egyptians were already using pictorial hieroglyphs prior to the birth of their nation around 3150 B.C. This finding is a shocking historical revelation. The finding of these hieroglyphs in a grave dated to this period strongly implies that:

1. The language existed before the Egyptian nation.
2. The Egyptian script is the first on earth.
3. Created by people who were not yet Egyptian.

Hieroglyphic tag found in Menes Tomb

Anu-Kushite Origin of the Egyptian Language

Some Egyptologist have implied that Menes was the creator of the Egyptian script. The reason for this theory is the fact that the tags were found in his tomb. This argument doesn't work for me on several levels.

The first reason I don't believe Menes created the Egyptian script is that he did not claim to have created it. Secondly, the tags were not hanging from Menes's neck as a representation of his ownership. The tags were used to label supplies used by the Pharaoh in his afterlife. The third reason I don't accept the argument that Menes created the script is that the tags were used commercially. Commercial use of these tags implies that this was a common practice that long preceded Menes.

Anu-Kushite Ownership of the Script

My theory states that if Anu-Kush is the origin of Egypt, then it is also the origin of the Egyptian language and script. I believe that a priestly Anu-Kushite sect created the Egyptian script in the distant past many years before Menes existed. The writing was considered sacred, and in the beginning, was used only by the priesthood. From this point forward, I'll refer to the formal version of the Anu-Egyptian script as the temple language.

Over time, the Kushite hierarchy decided to share the temple language with the general population because of its unique written component. The priest discovered that by sharing the temple language, you can extract commercial benefits and still retain its mystical characteristics. The sharing of the temple language also promoted linguistic, business, and national unity among the pre-Egyptian Anu-Kush.

While I believe that my argument for an Anu-Kushite origin of the Egyptian language is sound, it is the behavior of the Kush concerning the word that convinced me that my theory is correct. Other factors that lead me to believe that the Kushites invented the Egyptian language are:

1. The Anu-Kush as the majority culture after Menes, showed no resistance to the so-called Egyptian language.

2. The Anu-Kush clearly used the language in commerce before there was a formal nation of Egypt.

3. The Anu-Kush doggedly protected the old version of the original Egyptian temple language as I'll demonstrate later.

The above-listed actions are not behaviors one would expect from a people on behalf of a foreign language. If the Egyptian script was created by a culture other than the Anu-Kush, who is this culture? Where is their history of expertise, protection, and improvement of the writing?

Given the extensive history of Anu-Kushite trade practices, I can further speculate that the Anu-Kush used the Egyptian language in commerce because it already had a written form. Most of the tags found in Menes's tomb were for commercial use. If you already have a working written language, there is no incentive to create another from a local dialect. The Anu-Kushite affinity for the temple language is strong evidence that they created it.

Egyptian Script in the 25th Dynasty

During the early history of Egypt, some of the most significant literature was written in the old form created by Anu-Kushites. However, over time, the ancient structure was slowly substituted for a more modern version of the Egyptian script. But something extremely unusual occurred during the 25th dynasty.

The affinity for the ancient temple language was so intense among the Anu-Kush that immediately after conquering Egypt, they reinstated the old form of the word. The Kushites restored the old Egyptian style that had been abandoned by the previous Egyptian rulers. Why would the Anu-Kush do that?

The Anu-Kushites never claimed to be the origin of the Egyptian language. Yet, their protective behavior and dedication to the old temple language point firmly in this direction. Deduction and a mature understanding of human behavior reinforce my belief that the Anu-Kushite is the origin of the original Egyptian script.

The Kushite Meroitic Language

The Anu-Kushites were linguistic genesis! There is strong circumstantial evidence that the Anu-Kush created the Egyptian language. But the Anu-Kush didn't stop there. Seven hundred years after the 25th dynasty, the Anu-Kush created another unique language called the Meroitic script.

It was not until the reign of Kanteke Amani-shakheto (the scholar queen) in the late 1st Century BC that the Kushites decided to create a new script based on their native tongue. This period in Kushite history occurred after the Roman wars. By this time period, the Kushites were in renaissance and the Kemet, previously controlled by the Greeks, were no more.

At this time, the Kushites were becoming more nationalistic as a result of their negative experiences with the Greeks and Romans. By the first century BC, Kushites severed their ties with the Egyptians and more importantly, the old Egyptian script. The Kushites were entering the Meroitic renaissance period that drove them to new heights of cultural creativity.

Wall relief of the Candice Amani-shakheto

The Candice Amani-shakheto is referred to by historians as the Queen of the Meroitic Script. It was by her command that the Kushites created the Meroitic language. Archaeological findings from walls and stela dated from the Meroitic period show that the Kushites were a highly literate culture. Along with the Meroitic language, the Kushites also created a new form of hieroglyphics.

When the Kushites decided to create a new written language, they proved once again the absolute brilliance of their society. With the new Meroitic language, the Kushites added something revolutionary to world literacy that had never been seen before. The Kushites were the first on earth to divide their sentences into separate word phases using various symbols representing different types of pauses. This innovation made reading more comfortable and sped up the learning process for the general public.

The Kushites understood the importance of an educated population. They had already created and mastered two languages within their unique culture. But Kushite linguistic genius did not stop with sentence structure and punctuation.

The only alphabet on earth older than the Meroitic alphabet is the Greek alphabet created 750 B.C. While some signs and symbols of the Kushite script were borrowed from the earlier Egyptian language, overall, the Meiotic alphabet was unique. To date, the Meroitic language has not been completely deciphered. We do think that the Kushite script contained approximately 23 letters.

Understanding the Meroitic script would be incredibly valuable to our knowledge of the Kushite civilization. Unfortunately, the scholarly efforts aimed at deciphering the text are limited. Unless decoded, our most profound understanding of the Kushite kingdom and its people will remain theoretic.

Chapter 6: The Historical Kushite (Part 4)

The Many Manifestations of the Kush

The history of the Kush is both ancient and complicated. Faulty western interpretations have distorted Kushite history to reduce its relevance. Case in point: The Kushites defeated the Egyptians and reunited the lands of the two cobras. Egyptologist refers to this period as the so-called age of the Black Pharaohs. I use the euphemism (so-called) to dispute the assumption that before the Kushite conquest, Pharaohs were not black. I would argue that before the many Egyptian invasions, most of the legitimate Pharaohs of Egypt were of black African ancestry, as was the majority of the population.

What does the word Egypt Mean?

The word Egypt means black land. The Ancient Egyptians called their nation Kemet, which also means black with no reference to soil. I believe that Western archeologists purposely distorted the correct connotation of the word Egypt (Kemet). Europeans who were exploring the remains of Egypt alleged that the name Egypt or Kemet referred to its fertile black soil. This bios interpretation assumed that black people could not have created an advanced society like Kemet.

An enlightened observer would have recognized that the name Egypt, Kemet, and Sudan have the same meaning. The land of the black! In ancient times, the majority of Kemet (Egypt) was sand and rocky gravel. If the Egyptians named themselves referring to their soil type, they would have named Kemet sand. The definition of the word Kemet is a subtle but profound coincidence implying that the Kush (Sudan) and Egypt were, at some point, a singular national entity under the control of black Africans.

The Six Manifestations of the Kush

The Anu-Kushites are one of the oldest and least understood civilizations on earth. Because of the long timelines associated with the Kushite history, I have broken their history into six general periods or manifestations. These Kushite historical periods are labeled Neolithic, Napata, Meroitic, Nabatean X-Group, Greek/Roman, and Christian/Islamic. The first of these historical periods is the Neolithic, which began approximately 12,000 years ago.

The Neolithic Anu-Kushite

Kushite myth speaks of an ancient people who spread themselves throughout the world. There is a growing body of genetic evidence that implies that this may have occurred. When studying an unknown like the Kush, you must gather evidence from as many scientific disciplines as possible. This broad approach enables the analyzer to see relationships that might be impossible when viewing from a single perspective. An example is the use of phylogeny and linguistics in a comparison study. When phylogenetic studies are applied to the Kush, its results suggest a genetic link between Kushites of Africa and Kushites of Eurasia.

What does this mean? It could mean that this Afro-Eurasia relationship is coincidental. However, given the human migratory patterns from northeast African, coincidence is highly unlikely. These findings may also imply that there were two Kushite empires, both of which originated in Sudan. A third interpretation indicates that there was once a contiguous Anu-Kushite empire

that stretched from southeastern Africa to Eurasia.
Here is an excerpt from a study submitted to the Current Research Journal of Biological Sciences by Clyde A. Winters dated April 2010. This study is titled: Kushite Spread of Haplogroup R1*-M173 from Africa to Eurasia.

Winter states that "the phylogenetic profile of R-M173 supports an ancient migration of Kushites from the area of Sudan to West Africa and Eurasia as suggested by the classical writers."

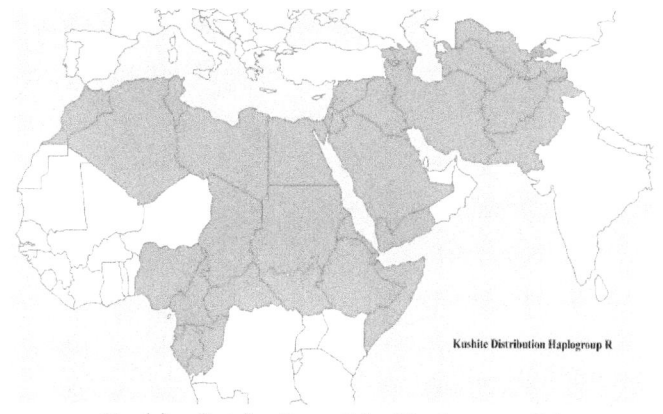

Kushite distribution of the Haplogroup R1.

"This expansion of an African or Anu-Kushite population probably took place in the Neolithic period. The map shown above represents the Kushite distribution of the Haplogroup R-1 coincide with further linguistic evidence that the Nilo-Saharan and Niger-Congo languages are related. The genetic evidence indicates that Nilo-Saharan and Niger-Congo speakers carry the y-chromosomes M3b*-M35 and R1*-M173, an indicator for the earlier presence of speakers of these languages in an original Nile Valley homeland."

"The distribution of the y-chromosome, specifically haplogroups in areas formerly occupied by the Kushite people of Asia reveal continuity between the ancient inhabitants of Anatolia, Mesopotamia, Persia, and Africa. The genetic pattern also indicates a significant Sub-Saharan male contribution to the populations presently situated in south-western Eurasia."

The above finding may also explain why much of southern Eurasian to this very day is referred to as the Hindu-Kush.

When studying the Neolithic Kushite, you should begin with what the Kushites considered to be their ancient homeland of Sudan. There would have been no Kemet to the north of the first cataract during this period. Recent expeditions in Sudan have uncovered primitive tools that were up to fifty thousand years old.

Wadi-Haifa in northern Sudan

A community called the Khormusan had emerged in the Wadi-Halfa area just beneath the modern Egyptian border with Sudan an estimated 25,000 years ago. The existence of this settlement is supported by a large number of surrounding burial sites dated to this period.

Anthropologist Fred Wendorf in 1974, discovered an essential prehistoric site in the Nile valley. The site is located in the Libyan desert north of the current Sudanese border with Egypt. Wendorf dated the site from 9000 to 11,000 years old. This community was named Nabta and may have existed at a time before the vast Saharan desertification.

The settlement of Nabta was very sophisticated. Researchers found well-built homes, wells, tools, and weapons. There were palaces, forts, and structures used for astronomy and manufacturing. These findings suggest that the Khormusan and the Nabta of Sudan created a complex and centralized society during the Neolithic period.

There was also the discovery of an 8000-year-old herding

community in Sudan called the Khartoum Mesolithic people. This community specialized in pottery. The Khartoum pottery was the most elegant and sophisticated ever found at a Neolithic site.

Pottery was often buried with the dead, demonstrating that the Anu-Egyptian tradition of burial with valuables had its origin in the land of the Kush. Since these early findings, many other ancient sites have been uncovered in Sudan.

Each discovery leads us closer to determining that there were sophisticated civilizations south of kemet very early in human history. There is ample archaeological evidence that as early as 5000 BC there was already a well-established culture centered

Khartoum Mesolithic Pottery

at a place known today as Old Dongola in Sudan. This pre-Kerma civilization settled along the western bank of the Nile River just below the third cataract.

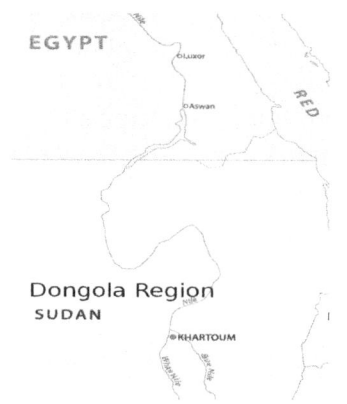

Map showing the Dongola Reach area of the Sudan

The Dongola settlement developed into a thriving city-state before 3500 BC. These pre-Kerma mega-cities were believed to be governed by a centralized authority with a fully functional organizational infrastructure similar to the Anu-Kush.

The ancient cities of the Dongola Reach were organized in a grid pattern like that of a modern city. This structural organization showed that a significant amount of planning went into the development of the city design. There is also evidence of ancient centers of administration and commerce. The cemeteries of old Dongola cities revealed a class-based burial structure and mortuary practices that were nearly identical to that of the pre-existing Anu.

Representation of Beehive Pyramid Burials at Dongola

What's astounding is that old Dongola is just one of several highly developed city-state systems located nearby that could have contributed to the building of the greater Kemet and Kushite Kingdoms. There are historical accounts of seven significant states in Kemet and Sudan. These Anu-Kushite tribes ranged from the Wawat in the north to the Yam in the south. All of these states appear to be of (Anu) black African origin.

The Yam, who originated from the southern Dongola Reach, became the strongest of the seven tribes. Sudanese historians believe that Yam eventually consumed the other six states forming the first Anu-Kushite nation. The date of the formation of the Anu-Kushite nation is unknown but is believed to have occurred prior to 6200 BC.

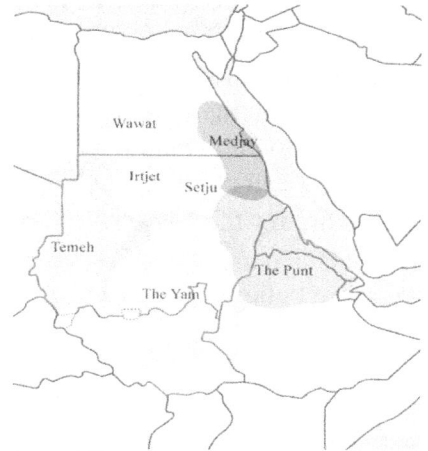

Location of the Seven Tribes of the Anu-Kush

Just three hours further north on the Nile from Old Dongola, is the location of the ancient Kushite city of Kerma. It is from the city of Kerma within the Dongola Reach, that the Kushites claim their origin. The Kushites were often called the Kerma people. There is evidence that the city-state of Kerma was established before 2600 BC and may have existed in a lesser form prior to the existence of Kemet. Kerma is also the most likely location of the Kushite capital during Egypt's war of independence in 3150 BC.

Map showing location of the ancient city of Kerma

The city of Kerma was incredibly sophisticated and held great wealth. The wealth of the Kushites is reflected in the well-preserved architecture. Below is an elaborate Kushite temple in Kerma called a Deffufa. There have only been three Deffufa temples found in all of Sudan, although it is assumed that there were many more. These temples were large, with some up to 20 meters in height and utterly unique to the Anu-Kush. Or are they? See chapter on Kushite architecture for the answer.

The Deffufas were believed to have been used as rooftop religious and astrological observatories. The Deffufas where solar temples dedicated to the transport of the soul through the night journey across the sky. The Deffufa temple shown below is thousands of years old and is severely eroded. The building design incorporated both stone and fired mud brick layering that has resulted in uneven weathering. Note the extensive structural bases around the Deffufa. These foundations suggest the existence of a highly sophisticated ancient city.

Kushite Western Deffufa Temple in Kerma city Complex

The wealth of the ancient Anu-Kush is reflected in the elaborate burials found at Kerma. Most Kushites were buried in simple ground-level tombs called the tumulus grave. Often, a stone bed platform was placed within the grave, and the body lay in a fetal position. Personal belongings and provisions for the afterlife were placed around the dead, suggestive of later Egyptian burials.

A Stone or Mud brick Mustaba Tomb

The next development in burial design was called a Mastabas shown above. The Mastaba is a grave dug in the ground and covered by a low stone or mud-brick rectangular tomb.

Many Kushite burial sites at Kerma contained jewelry, weapons, and artifacts from around the known world. These findings support the belief that the Kushites prior to 2600 BC were performing a vast amount of trade with populations in sub-Saharan Africa, the Levant, the Red Sea region, and multiple Mediterranean communities.

Gold ring found in Karma burial site

Please note that the ring shown above is representing the King of Kush. The King is wearing the double crown of the two cobras. This ring implies that this Kushite King or Queen reigned over the two lands of the cobra, upper and lower Kush. The ring reinforces my theory that Kush and Egypt were of a singular Anu origin.

The early Kerma governing system was used as the foundation for the next phase of Kushite social evolution, which is called the Napatan period.

The Napatan Kushite

The second manifestation of the Kush is called the Napata period. The Napatan period is dated from approximately 900 BC to 540 BC. During this period, the Kush reached the height of its territorial expansion. The Anu-Kush dominated the Nile valley from the Delta to the borders of what is now Uganda. The Kush conquered Egypt during this period and expanded its northern empire to the Kingdom of Palestine.

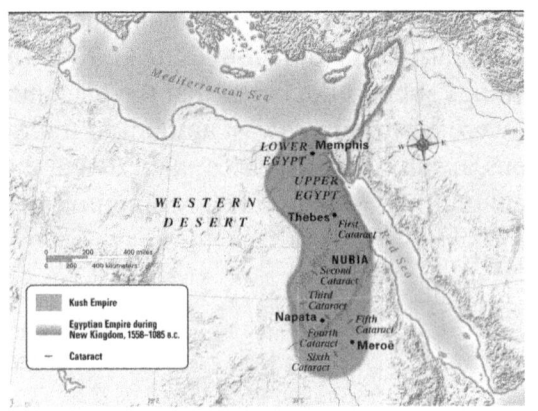

Kushite Conquest during Napata period

The Napata period is called this became Napata became the principal (capital city) of the Kushite Kingdom. Old Napata is located forty minutes north of Khartoum.

During the Napata period, the most important religious site for the Kush was Jebel Barkal, located in northern Sudan at the third cataract of the Nile. Jebel Barkal was considered a religious shrine by the Anu-Kush since the Neolithic age. This mountain was believed by the Kush and the Kemet to house the creator God Amun. The Kushites described Amun as having the heart of a Lion and the hair of a Ram.

Aerial view over Mt. Jebel Barkal

It was during the Napata period that the Kushites took complete control of Egypt. The person responsible for the conquest of Kemet was the Kushite Pharaoh Piankhi (Pi). We will discuss the Pharaoh Piankhi and the conquest of Egypt later in this text.

Post war Kushite control of Kemet lasted approximately two hundred years. During this period Kemet experienced relative peace and prosperity. There were five official Kushite Pharaohs of the 25th dynasty named in the list of Kushite Kings. However, I have discovered that there were more than five post-war Kushite pharaohs who reigned for at least one hundred years longer than they are credited.

The Kushite Napata period was also a time of incredible architectural advancement in the land of the two cobras. The Kushites built many temples in various locations within the combined Kingdom that were of both typical Kemet and uniquely Kushite design.

Meroitic Periods of the Kushite Nation

The third manifestation of the Kush is called the first Meroitic period. The Meroitic period is subdivided into four segments. The first Meroitic period is dated from approximately 540 BC to 370 BC. The first Meroitic period launched the second Kushite renaissance. The Meroitic period is called this because the Kush moved their administrative capital to the city of Meroe in Sudan.

This Meroitic period also saw an explosion in Kushite art, linguistics, architecture, and military prowess. One of the best-known Kushite Kings of this period was Arkamani-qo, whose pyramid is located in the old city of Meroe.

Pyramid of King Arkamaniqo and other royal tombs

During the four Meroitic phases, the Kushite Kings rule from both Napata and Meroe. The main temple of Amun is still in Napata, while the new temple of Amun in Meroe is under construction. During this period, the majority of Kushite royalty is being buried in the city of Nuri.

The Nabatan X-Group 4th Manifestation

Meroitic Phase 2 occurred after 370 BC. The primary Kushite seat of power was moved to the city of Meroe, and royal families prefer to be buried there. Napata is still religiously relevant and is the location of the old Amun Temple.

During this period, the Kushites began to experience a gradual decline in power. While still a regional force, the golden age of the Kushites was beginning to wane. The Kushite kingdom was suffering increased numbers of nomadic invasions and a weakening central government. Kushite border territories were also under threat with an ever-weakening response from Kushite leadership.

The Kushites believed that the Kingdom's problems stemmed from those who no longer followed the Ma'at. One of the most powerful of the non-Ma'atic nomad tribes were called the Nabo (Nabatean). The Nabatean group slowly occupied Kushite lands in the Nile Valley, resulting in a weakening of the Kushite state. The Kush was also under siege by a number of splinter nations to its east. These nations would later come to be known as Axum, Eritrea, and Abyssinia.

As Kushite power waned, the Nabo people moved into the area of the second cataract and formed a cohesive community with the Kush. This new community was the genesis for what the scientist would designate as the Nabatan X-Group.

The Nabo did not follow the Kushite/Kemet tradition of pyramid burials. Instead, the Nabo returned to the old tumulus form of burial seen several thousand years earlier. In 332 BC, another invader was fragmenting the Kemet state called the Greeks. The Greeks dominated the Kemet primarily in the northern delta region. It is important to note that the Greeks were never able to dominate or defeat the Kushites in the south.

Over time, the Greeks, Nabo, and the remaining Kush fragmented into three weaker kingdoms that would set the stage for the arrival of the Roman Kushite era in 30 BC.

The Roman Kushite Era - 5th Manifestation

The Meroitic Phase 3 period began at the time of the Roman invasion of Kemet in approximately 30 BC. The Kushite seat of government and royal palaces are now primarily located in the imperial city of Meroe, which was also now the chosen location for royal burials. The city of Meroe flourishes with numerous building projects. The Kushites also attempted to isolated themselves from Roman influence in the north. The Candice Queen Amani-Renas, also known as the warrior Queen, would neutralize the Roman military threat from the north. Her sister Amani-Shakheto would rule the Kush after Amanirenas, and she instituted a new Meroitic writing system during this period.

By 100 AD, the once vast kingdom of Kush has fragmented into several nation-states controlled from Meroe. While the heart of Kush remained Kush, the territory was falling under the control of its tribal descendants. One of the most powerful of these ancestral Anu-Kushite descendants was the Axumites. The country of Axum arose around 100 AD and existed until approximately 600 AD. Axum originated on the eastern red sea coast of the old kingdom of Kush. Ethiopia was also a child of the Anu-Kush, and it also became a separate nation in the first century AD.

While Kush still controlled southern Kemet and the Dongola reach, their power was being challenged on all sides. Kushite territory was also being contested by a desert people known as the Bedouins. Bedouin tribes had existed since the time of the Kushite conquest of Egypt. However, the weakening state of the Kushite nation made the Bedouin a far greater threat.

Christianity was introduced to the Kushites in the 3rd century AD in two ways. The first occurred via gradual interaction and marriage with other ethnic groups in Kemet that had adopted Christianity. The other and more substantial source of Christianity come from the ethnic children of the Kush called the Abyssinian, also known as the Ethiopian.

Era of Islamic Expansion – 6th Manifestation

The sixth manifestation and 4th phase of the Meroitic Kushite period began in the late third century AD and continued until the fall of the Kushite nation in the early 6th century. This late Kushite period witnessed the slow demise and cultural twilight of the Meroitic Kushite. During this period, Kushites in Egypt and, to a lesser extent, Sudan, was being compromised by outside cultures. Commerce and war were the primary reasons for these cultural challenges. These unavoidable cultural pressures also included challenges to the old religion of the Kush by a new middle eastern faith called Islam.

The fall of the formal Kushite nation in Sudan occurred in approximately 630 AD. However, the Kushites didn't just disappear. The Muslim conquest of Egypt began shortly after the Kushite demise in the year 639 AD. Several of the existing pockets of ethnic tribes in Kemet had already accepted Islam. With the invasion of Egypt and North Africa, Islam was well on its way to becoming the new dominant religion in this region.

Islam was introduced to the children of Kush several years before the Islamic invasion of Egypt. Islam was already a religious force in the lives of several Kushite and Bedouin tribes as a result of both trade, marriage and peaceful Islamic evangelicalism. Muslim groups also settled in Kemet and Kush, and these communities grew peacefully among the Christians. In 641AD, the Muslim expansion across North Africa began with the Arab invasion of Egypt.

West Africa was introduced to Islam in the 9th century AD. The continent of Africa is now the home to one-quarter of the world's Muslim population. I have argued in previous chapters that the Kush is the origin of the Egyptian culture and language. The Kush also remained Egypt's primary population throughout the first 2500 years of its existence. In ancient times, Egypt was invaded or commercially integrated by the Hyksos, Libyans, Assyrians, Persians, the Levant, Bedouins, Greeks, Romans, and finally, the Arabs. None of these foreign cultures can claim to be the origin of Kemet, with the exception of the Kush.

The day the Kushites were destroyed militarily in the 6th century, was not the final day for their culture or the old religion of the Pharaohs. Despite the expansion of Islam, most Kushites were either Christian or remained loyal to the ancient faith of the Pharaohs for many years to come. It took another one thousand years for Islam to spread throughout Sudan and Western Africa. What is clear is that the Arab invasion of Egypt explains the current population that exists there today.

Chapter 7: The Religion of the Kush

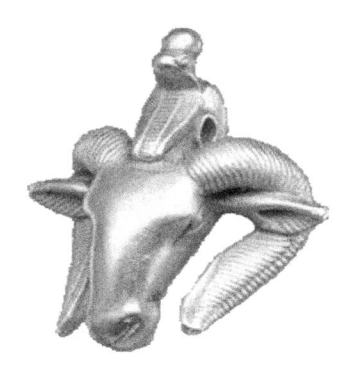

Kushite Doctrine of Human Decency

The Anu-Kush is one of the oldest civilizations on earth and often referred to itself as the long-lived Kush. In my discussion of the Kush, I divide them into three distinctive categories. These categories are racial (ethnic Anu-Kush - black African), cultural Kush (religious), and the national Kush, (the political systems of the Anu-Kush/Kemet states).

Placing the Kushite into these three categories enables us to see the Kush as they actually were, an ancient and sophisticated people in evolution. I believe that the failure of the western interpretation of African history lay in their inability to see black people as they see themselves, a people who evolve with time.

While some say the religious history of the Kushite is obscure, I would strongly disagree. The spiritual obscurity some are referring to is, in reality, a misinterpretation of the available evidence. My argument is simple. Everything religious in this region of Africa during the Neolithic period, 12,000 years ago, to the time of the first Christians, had its origin in the ethnic Anu. If you can accept this single reality supported by anthropological evidence, the origin of everything human in this region becomes obvious.

Are the Anu the Origin of Kemetic Faith?

The truth is, I have no idea if the Anu-Kush were the origin of the Kemetic faith. However, there is ample circumstantial evidence that an ethnic Anu origin is most probable. The archaeologist has speculated that the Anu-Kush was practicing the precursors of the pharaoh-based faith more than 6,000 years ago. Much of this speculation is based on the burial rituals of the Anu at this remote period in history. Keep in mind that religion and burial practices often go hand-in-hand.

Ancient burials in the Dongola region of Sudan also hint at the religious contribution of the ethnic Anu to the Kemet/Kushite faith. These similarities in funeral practices are tantalizing evidence of an ethnic Anu origin. Yes, these burial practices did change over time. For example, while the tumulus grave was common both above and below the first cataract of the Nile, they subtly changed with time. For example, the position of the bodies changed from face-down to face-up to fetal. These subtle changes in burial position can occur without the influence of an outside source.

Gravesites Before Menes's Tomb

Menes, the first Pharaoh of Egypt, is not the only pre-dynastic tomb found at Abydos in the local cemetery at Umm el-Qa'ab. There is evidence, as claimed by the Kush, that there were many pre-dynastic Kings that ruled over various city-states before there was a Kemet. The Anu-Kush claim that these pre-dynastic Kings preceded known Egyptian rulers by as much as 3000 years.

An example of Kings that preceded Menes was King Iry-Hor and King Ka, who ruled in 3200 BC. The discovery of the tombs of these pre-dynastic Kings suggests that there was a long history of pre-Kemet ethnically Anu Kings in this region.

The burial of the pre-dynastic Kings were more elaborate examples of the old tumulus style grave. In 5000 BC, the Kerma culture was already demonstrating sophisticated burial practices similar to the Kemet. The Kerma Kush also used the tumulus and several other unique burial styles.

The simple tumulus style begins with the digging of a round or rectangular pit. Depending on social rank, a smooth stone bed might be placed in the grave. Some graves were outlined in mud or fire brick on the interior or exterior. The body of the deceased is laid upon the stone base or ground in a fetal position facing east.

Ancient stone tumulus burials at Kerma 2450 B.

Even simple tumulus graves were often surrounded by religious objects, gifts, jewelry, weapons, and pottery. Because the Egyptian was of the same ethnic origin of the Kush, you would expect these practices to reveal themselves in later Egyptian burial practices.

The tombs of Menes and other pre-dynastic Kings, while more substantial than the ordinary tumulus grave, matched its basic Anu-Kushite style, content, and description. One rank related difference was that the King's tombs usually contained a second room for the storage of food and treasure.

Open Menes's tomb at Abydos.

The Pharaoh Menes tomb contained the artifacts one would expect in an Anu-Kushite burial. Menes's tomb was encased in fired mud brick and included an additional room for storage of materials used in the afterlife. Menes's tomb was smaller than that of previous Kings despite his designation as the first Pharaoh of Egypt.

The Many Gods of the Kush

The Anu-Kushite and the Anu-Kemet shared many Gods and religious traditions. The origin of the Gods is more difficult to determine. At the time of the first Pharaoh Menes, I suspect that religious beliefs of the ethnic Kush and the newly formed Kemet would have been identical. Logically, Religious distinctions between the two national groups would be expected to diverge over time.

What is obvious is that the Kemet and the Kush worshipped the same Gods, sometimes under different names. The two nations also placed a different degree of importance on various Gods. These religious differences in no way changes my belief that their religions had a common origin.

The Anu-Kushite religion was a multi-deity faith with each God possessing a specific type of physical and/or personality-based attribute. The Gods themselves lived in a world of order where each was given a divine rank and purpose. The Gods were also known to have two or more names and could appear in several eclectic forms.

The senior God of the Kush/Kemet was the God Amun and was widely understood to be the creator God. Other Gods possessed other traits many of which were bestowed upon man during the creation process.

Introduction to Anu-Kushite Gods

The Anu-Kushite religion contained a pantheon of unusual yet meaningful Gods. The most important of these Gods is **Amun**. Amun was depicted in several forms including that of the sitting ram. For the Kush, the primary physical form of Amun was a man with a human body and the head of a ram. He is carrying the royal staff indicating his prerogative to choose the ruler of the Kushite and Egyptian Kingdom.

The Kushite God **Amun** was believed by the Kush to be the father of earth and the creator of mankind. He is described as having the heart of a lion and the hair of a ram. Temples to the God Amun were built all over the Kushite Kingdom. One of the largest of the Kushite Amun temples was located at the sacred mountain of Jebel Barkal. Amun also acted as a guide to Kushite leadership and as protector of the people.

The Anu Goddess **Isis** played an essential part in Kushite religious mythology. Her role among the Kush was as a mother figure who protected women in childbirth. The cult of Isis was one of the most popular in all of Kush. Among the Kush, Isis has often been depicted suckling the infant Kushite king in her arms. The Kushite Goddess Isis wears the royal crown of the hawk.

Isis was known among the Kushites as the Great Lady often claimed by kings to be their divine mother. This claim was usually made to establish a divine connection to legitimize power. The Goddess Isis also promoted high moral standards, especially among women, and she was the guardian of the underworld.

While Isis was revered among the Kush as the mother God, the God of protection in motherhood was the Goddess **Bastet**.

The Goddess Bastet began life as a lioness God of war. She was known for her fierceness in battle and was used as the patron saint by several of the Kushite warrior queens. Later in Kushite history, Bastet evolved into the cat Goddess and protector. Her cult encouraged female athleticism, expertise with weapons, ointments and other forms of magical protection.

The Kushite God **Apedemak** played a significant role in the religious life of the Kush. Apedemak is the Kushite Lion God of war. Among the Kushites, he was often associated with the various manifestations of the moon.

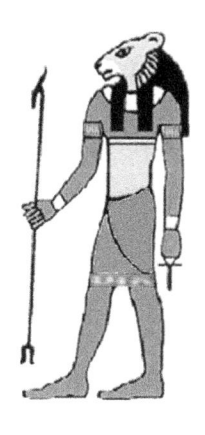

The God Apedemak appears in human form with the head of a lion and the staff of royal lineage. Apedemak accompanied the Kushite warrior into battle for more than 5,000 years. The Kushites were never defeated in that time, and the fierceness of Apedemak was the reason why. This God symbolizes power, strength, and courage.

Next in our Kushite pantheon of Gods is **Anubis**. He is the God of the underworld who ushers souls into the afterlife. This is a very old God that appeared in Kushite religious lure as early as 3200 B.C. The God Anubis appears as a man-wolf hybrid.

The God Anubis most often appears as a wolf-headed man carrying the royal staff. It is believed that the Kushite picked the wolf because of the native African golden wolf that was sacred to the Kush. Anubis was also known as the God of judgment because he attends the scale of justice. Anubis was usually shown with deep black skin to depict the purity of his relationship to the Royals.

The God **Osiris** is known as the God of the afterlife and/or the underworld. He was believed to be forever young. The pharaohs referred to Osiris as the silent lord, a title they would use on special religious occasion. The God Osiris is most often depicted as a partially mummified green skinned pharaoh holding the crook and frail.

Osiris wears the distinctive double crown of Egypt. Osiris was the ruler of the western slope of the Nile or land of the dead. It was believed that as Osiris rose each day, so would the sun and both would enjoy eternal life.

One of the oldest and most revered of the ancient Gods of Kush is the deity **Horus**. The mythology of this God describes him as the son of Isis and Osiris. He is also described as Ra, the son of the Sun God.

The God Horus acts as the protector of the Pharaoh. He is most often represented as a man with the head of a falcon or as a falcon with protective wings hovering over the shoulders of the pharaoh. It is not clear if there were any differences in how the Kushites viewed Horus when compared to the Egyptian.

There are few skills more important to Kushites than those associated with education and literature. The ability to write (the Scribe) played a critical role in the development of the Kushite society. The skill of the scribe was controlled by the god **Thoth**. While government employed scribes were writing the most elaborate works of literature, ordinary people were also encouraged to learn to read and write. The Kush understood that it could not sustain a viable kingdom without expanding literacy to everyone.

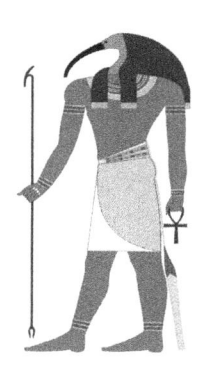

The God **Thoth** gave the Kushite the ability to create and master language and science. He also gave us the glorious gift of wisdom. Thoth was depicted as a man with the head of an Ibis. He is the husband of the Goddess Ma'at. Thoth and his wife the Ma'at stood on either side of the Ra's boat (solar universe) keeping it and the universe in perfect balance.

There are few topics more important to the Kushite than the divine practice of commerce. Business was the centerpiece of Kushite life. Commerce acted as the engine of the nation, and every citizen should be involved. The Kushites believed that they were able to build their great wealth as a result of attributes they received from the God **Ptah**.

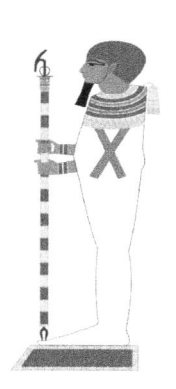

The Kushite God Ptah usually appears as a small man covered with feathers. He is responsible for giving the Kushite craftsmanship, artistic talent, and exceptional merchant skills. This God ties in well with the Kushite concept of the God phase, also known as the creative stage of life. The Kushite must train themselves in every manner possible to create an enterprise.

The Goddess **Sekhmet** was known as a warrior and healer. She was also associated with anger and chaos. She is the female version of the arch God Chaos.

Sekhmet is often referred to as the daughter of Ra. She wears the sun-disk and the uraeus which depicts both her royalty and her power. Sekhmet is the strangest of all the Gods because like her male counterpart Chaos, she existed before time. It was out of Chaos that all things were formed. However, it was Chaos in his rivalry with Amun that bestowed chaos upon mankind.

In the day-to-day life of a Kushite, there was no God more important than the Goddess **Ma 'at**. The Ma 'at is the Kushite Goddess of harmony, peace, and justice. The Kushites rightfully believed that the Ma 'at, also referred to as the Mother Ma 'at, was the true protector of man. The Kush also believed that the divine protection provided by a consistent morality was even more powerful than that of the sword and bow.

The Ma 'at tells us that peace is generated by the individual and dispersed among the people. Each person is both the origin and center of their words and deeds. It is our words and deeds that set into motion a world of harmony or a world of chaos. Without justice, chaos rules and nothing good will be accomplished. Harmony is threatened by chaos and chaos is nurtured by immorality.

The Tenets of the Ma'at

The miraculous rules of harmony bestrewed upon humanity is called the Tenets of the Ma'at. These tenets are simple moral doctrines of human decency that direct how we should treat one another. The Ma'at does not care about a person's external individuality.

Your politics, tribe, race, or religion means nothing to the Ma'at. The Ma'at does not exempt itself, nor the faith of its origin, from the rules of human decency.

The Ma'at addresses moral behavior rather than just moral thought. While the Ma'at wants you to be genuinely moral and will direct you on that path, only you can make that choice. Choosing the way of the Kush (tenets of the Ma'at) is the more natural path of life and will lead to both personal and social harmony.

The Ma'at does not care what you think or feel; it cares only about how you speak and treat others. To the Ma'at, you are the center of the universe, alive and in your God Phase. During this phase, it is you who is responsible for both the good and evil you create. The warriors of the Ma'at must come to believe that it is his/her personal morality that will determine if Chaos prevails.

The moral code of the Kush demands that each individual elevate themselves in the realization that you are a vital cog in the machinery of harmony. It cannot happen without you! The Ma'at can give you guidance in what morality looks like, but it cannot make you moral. The Ma'at encourages you to accept the pursuit of justice as your core value, and whispers these words into the souls of humanity:

> "The strength and effectiveness of any virtue is determined by the consistency of its application!"

Other Gods of the Kush

There are other gods in the Kushite pantheon, such as Sebiumeker, the Gatekeeper God, and Bes the God of pleasure. Bes is said to have given humanity the appreciation and talent for singing and dancing. There were Gods of fertility and Gods of the mountains. There were crocodile Gods and Gods of air and water. While I want you to be aware of these lesser gods, they are only mildly relevant to the remainder of this presentation.

Who is the God Chaos?

In Anu-Kushite and Anu-Kemetic mythology, Chaos is the God responsible for disharmony, disorder, violence, and destruction. The key to defeating Chaos lay in understanding what it is. The goal of Chaos is to destroy humanity to demonstrate the incompetence of his chief rival Amun. If humanity perishes from the face of the earth, this will signify the inferiority of Amun and his most heralded creation, humankind. The self-destruction of humanity would place into doubt Amun's worthiness to hold the title of Supreme God.

Chaos was the first of the deities and from him sprang all other Gods. For this reason, Chaos believed himself to be supreme among the heavenly Lords. However, when put to the vote, the other deities chose Amun because of his balance of virtues. This action infuriated Chaos and set into motion an undeclared war between the two.

This rivalry led Chaos to use every force at his disposal to cause the extinction of mankind. Since the day of enlightenment, Chaos has inflicted humanity with endless turmoil, fear, conflict, and destruction. Chaos has also set into motion a war of virtue that, if not won, will result in the total annihilation of humankind.

What is Chaos?

Chaos is distrust, willful ignorance, violence, entitlement, bigotry, lies, and the acceptance of evil. Chaos is universally known as the demon or devil god, although he has many other names. Chaos resides within the mind of every human being, and his influence is inescapable.

If you look deep into the soul of Chaos, you'll discover the actual reason for his hatred of Amun and humankind. Chaos knew in his heart that he was not worthy of being the Supreme God because he lacked virtue. It was Chaos's envy and lack of morality that fueled his hatred for Amun. Humanity is the vehicle used by Chaos to attack and destroy Amun, his arch-rival.

Those who are corrupted by Chaos are called the Apepa (the evil or corrupt). The Apepa is the physical manifestation of evil and the servant of Chaos. The Apepa enables Chaos to degrade the quality of human life by injecting distrust, conflict, and endless rivalries into the world.

Chaos functions through his minions who persuade, seduce, or intimidate others into evil acts. Each heinous act performed by an Apepa injects disharmony into the lives of humanity.

Every human being is potentially an Apepa (minion of Chaos). People decide for themself if he/she will embrace or reject evil. The Kush believed that free-will is an intricate part of human creativity, but it also creates the opportunity to choose evil over good. You cannot force a person to accept virtue. Laws or the threat of violence do not stop people from robbing, coveting, cheating, and killing one another. Only the internal acceptance of virtue can control the evil within. Chaos can only be defeated by virtue, which is always a personal choice.

Does Chaos Really Exist?

It was science and not religion that enabled this elder to recognize the existence of the demon Chaos. In science, if you want to prove that something exists, you create an equation or an experiment that test the essence of your hypothesis. The essence of Chaos is disorder. If your experiments show a predictable relationship between cause and effect, you have proven your theory. Add more chaos to any circumstance and the effect will be more disorder. Just as the demon Chaos promised, in our universe, all things move to disorder.

A strange little man named Issac Newton came to exist in England in the 1700s. It was he who identified the second law of thermodynamics that also strangely defines Chaos. Newton called this state of expanding disorder entropy, where everything moves in the direction of Chaos.

Place a teacup on a counter, and it will appear unchanged or in a state of equilibrium. The unseen reality is that the cup is degrading right before your eyes within a time frame to slow for you to perceive. Add a chaotic force to the cup by pushing it onto the floor, and you will immediately see the effects of Chaos. Your forceful action will damage the cup, resulting in a faster state of depreciation and decay. The same is true of all actions based on good or evil. Actions both good and evil are a force that directly affect the quality of life in this world.

Chaos gave humanity the curse of perpetual disorder. All things, including our lives, the world, and the universe are destined to move in the direction of Chaos. Chaos is the reason why we and everything else in our world ages and dies. The best we can do is use our morality, wisdom, and courage to reduce or delay the destructive effects of Chaos.

Religion in Kushite Government

It's ironic that after seven thousand years, the relationship between government and religion is precisely the same.

Governments and religions are competitive and antagonistic. They are antipathetic because each covets the power of the other. The government leaders want the loyalty and absoluteness that comes from worshiping gods, while religion wants the ability to manipulate the lives of others, not necessarily associated with their faith.

Government and religious rivalry have been with the Kush since the beginning. However, the Kush used a unique solution to this common problem. To address this rivalry and keep it from causing disharmony, the Kush turned to the Ma 'at, the code of human decency.

The code of human decency defines how one person should treat another regardless of rank, appearance, faith, etc. The Ma 'at judges you only by your actions with respect to others, eliminating the behavioral excuses common with dogmatic beliefs. The Ma 'at enabled the Kush to strategically assign power to the various factions while reducing their ability to harm the population. The Ma 'at acted as a social buffer to protect the public from becoming the victims of government or religious extremes.

Sharing Power with Religion

The Kushites discovered from their own experience that Religion is a rival for government power. The Kush realized that allowing Religion to have a direct hand in government was unwise. The Kush did allow a state religion to dominate, but only with the Ma 'at as its caveat.

The Kush did not give the state religion the power to act against other persons, members, or faiths. The Kush understood that Religion consists of people who believe in a specific doctrine or dogma. Theology is concerned with meeting the needs of its believers and will cast out or attack all others. This tendency to religiously exclude or compete is the Achilles heel of religious doctrine.

Governments don't have the option of casting out citizens who disagree, although they often try. A government must meet the needs of all of its people, or risk being violently attacked. There has rarely been a successful religious government that did not also provide a secular justice system to protect the citizen from both. Secular justice is especially crucial in societies where there are many religious and or ethnic minorities.

Religion can be incompatible with the government because both want the same thing for very different reasons. A good government wants to promote a peaceful and prosperous nation, while a good religion intends to support itself. In helping itself, religions will eventually attack or deny access to those who are not their members.

Unfortunately, the above is the reason why neither Government nor Religion is the solution to world peace. The Kushites realized the flews of both government and Religion. The Kush demonstrated this wisdom by using the Ma 'at to define the moral limits of both.

Did the Kemet use the Ma 'at?

The Ma 'at remained a substantial part of Anu-Kemet society after their war of independence from the Kush. The Ma 'at promoted harmony between Kemet and the Kush after the battle of liberation. For approximately fourteen hundred years after the Egyptian war of independence, there was a religious synergy between the Anu-Kush and the Anu-Kemet. However, this spiritual synergy began to deteriorate as a result of the coming foreign rule of Egypt.

Around 1600 BC, northern Egypt was invaded by a people known as the Hyksos. The Hyksos were a Sematic people who practiced the religion of Baal. The Hyksos populated northern Egypt for over one hundred years and added to the ethnic and religious evolution of the native Kemet people. We know the origin of the Hyksos from the names of their Kings installed as pharaohs after Egypt's defeat.

Please note that the Hyksos did not conquer the Kush. The Hyksos did not even dominate the entire nation of Egypt. The Hyksos dominated the northern delta region as the indigenous Kemet leadership fled south to middle Egypt.

The Egyptians of this time found themselves living between two powerful groups, the Hyksos in the north and the Anu-Kushite in the south.

The Hyksos ruled over the majority of the Egyptian population and profoundly affected their culture and religion. The historical opinion is that the Hyksos were fairly good governors and added stability to Egypt. While the Hyksos accepted Egypt's religious traditions, they also deemphasized social behavior as directed by the Ma 'at. It is believed that the success of the Hyksos infuriated the native Egyptian leadership, assuring future conflict.

The Hyksos and the Ma 'at

The Hyksos was the first of many tribes to conquer Kemet. As the influence of the Hyksos expanded in lower Egypt, it slowly changed the Egyptian religious emphasis. The Ma 'at became less important to the Kemet but did not disappear. The indigenous Kemet leadership moved to the middle region of the country and began resisting the Hyksos, and the religious changes they championed.

While the Egyptian state under Hyksos domination was adequate, it had become more of an income-generating enterprise than a promoter of ethical behavior. For this reason, the indigenous Egyptian leadership rebelled against and eventually defeated the Hyksos.

The Kemet who defeated the Hyksos and retook the north, did not accomplish this feat by themselves. It was with the military cooperation of the Kush that enabled the Kemet to finally dislodge the Hyksos from control of their land.

The Ma 'at and Human Behavior

Religion has been a useful tool in controlling the lesser impulses of humankind for millennia. However, because of the political character of organized religion, it is subject to the same level of corruption as a government.

Denominations are in a position to control lives, wealth, and power. These elements tend to corrupt religious leadership, cloud their morality and their purpose. What began in the heart of the priest as a quest for social harmony can quickly evolve into a pursuit of power and wealth. Suddenly, faith is no longer focused on moral behavior but on how to fulfill some political or economic agenda.

The Anu-Kush did not want to confront religion and risk social upheaval. The Kushites felt it better to incorporate faith into the nation's cycle of influence quietly. This approach gave religion an unofficial voice in the direction of the country while limiting its dogmatic tendencies.

The Kush supported the alliance of government and religion by building temples, contributing funds to temple cults, awarding limited authority to priest, and gave the faith an official social status. These actions pacified the priest and purchased their cooperation. While the Anu-Kemet and the Anu-Kush were religious by nature, they were also pragmatic.

The most important religious influence of the Anu-Kush and the Anu-Kemet was the Ma'at, not the book of the dead as Egyptologists would have you believe. The Ma'at, also known as the code of human decency, focused on moral behavior. You could correctly refer to the Ma'at as the Kushite and Kemetic Book of the Living. The Ma'at was used as a guide to proper social etiquette and existed several millennia before the bible. I believe that the Ma'at was one of the sources of biblical ideology, including the ten commandments. The following is a list of the 42 Tenets of the Ma'at, the Anu-Kushite Doctrine of Human Decency.

Source of the Ten Commandments

It should be obvious that anything that came before can have a profound influence on that which comes after. The Ma'at existed before the bible and was shared and understood by those who would become the Hebrew. Therefore, it should not be surprising that the Ma'at influenced the theology of the Jewish faith. Did not the Jewish faith guide the creation of both Islam and Christianity? The answer is a resounding yes! So, did the Ma'at guide the ten tenets of Judaism? Let's do a comparison test of this hypothesis!

Kushites and Kemet used the tenets of the Ma'at as a prey recited twice a day. In the morning, the believer would tell the Gods of his or her intent for the day. For example, I will not lie, cheat or steal from others. In the evening, the believe would resight and remind the Gods of his action on that day. For example, I have not lied, cheated or stolen.

Here is a list of the forty-two tenants of the Ma'at. Each tenet represented by a God who is monitoring your behavior throughout your life.

1. I have not committed sin.
2. I have not committed robbery or violence.
3. I have not stolen.
4. I have not slain men or women.
5. I have not stolen food.
6. I have not swindled offerings to God/Goddess.
7. I have not stolen from God/Goddess.
8. I have not told lies.
9. I have not carried away food.
10. I have not cursed.
11. I have not closed my ears to truth.
12. I have not committed adultery.
13. I have not made anyone cry.
14. I have not felt sorrow without reason.
15. I have not assaulted anyone.
16. I have not been deceitful.
17. I have not stolen anyone's land.

18. I have not been an eavesdropper.
19. I have not falsely accused anyone.
20. I have not been angry without reason.
21. I have not seduced anyone's wife or husband.
22. I have not polluted myself.
23. I have not terrorized anyone.
24. I have not disobeyed the Law.
25. I have not been exclusively angry.
26. I have not cursed God/Goddess.
27. I have not behaved with violence.
28. I have not caused disruption of peace.
29. I have not acted hastily or without thought.
30. I have not overstepped my boundaries of concern.
31. I have not exaggerated my words when speaking.
32. I have not worked or encouraged evil.
33. I have not used evil thoughts, words or deeds.
34. I have not polluted the water.
35. I have not spoken angrily or arrogantly.
36. I have not cursed anyone in thought, word or deed.
37. I have not placed myself on a pedestal.
38. I have not forsaken the God/Goddess.
39. I have not stolen from or disrespected the deceased.
40. I have not taken food from a child.
41. I have not acted with insolence.
42. I have not destroyed property belonging to others.

Now let's compare the tenants of the Ma 'at with the Ten Commandments:

Commandment 1: I am the lord thy God. Thou shalt not have strange Gods before me.

The Ma 'at 38: I have not forsaken the lord thy God/Goddess.

Commandment 2: Thou shall not take the name of the lord thy God in vain.

The Ma 'at 26: I have not cursed God/Goddess.

Commandment 3: Keep holy the sabbath.

Ma 'at 6: I have not swindled offerings to God/Goddess.

Commandment 4: Honor thy father and thy mother.

The Ma 'at 37, 41: I have not acted with insolence or placed myself on a pedestal.

Commandment 5: Thou shalt not kill.

Ma 'at 4: I have not slain men or women.

Commandment 6: Thou shalt not commit adultery.

Ma 'at 21: I have not seduced anyone's wife or husband.

Commandment 7: Thou shalt not steal.

Ma 'at 2, 3: I have not stolen, robbed or committed violence.

Commandment 8: Thou shalt not bear false witness against thy neighbor.

The Ma 'at 19: I have not falsely accused anyone.

Commandment 9: Thou shalt not covet thy neighbor's wife.

The Ma 'at 21: I have not seduced anyone's wife or husband.

Commandment 10: Thou shalt not covet thy neighbor's goods.

The Ma 'at 2, 3, 5, 9, 20, 34: I have not stolen from anyone, not even the dead.

For those of you who would contest my belief in the origin of the ten commandments, please consider this. Moses was an adopted member of the Egyptian royal family. The Ma 'at was known to even the poorest of Egyptians. Therefore, there should be no doubt that Moses was very much aware of the 42 tenets of the Ma 'at. The knowledge of the Ma 'at alone would have been enough to influence Moses's version of the ten commandments. I do not contest that God inspired Moses to create the commandments. I'm simply pointing out that the Ma 'at was a significant influence, if not the direct source of these ten sacred tenets.

The Ma 'at and the Concept of Honor

The Kush believed that the kingdom of heaven is located one gate north of honor. Honor is the courage to do what's right, no matter what the consequence! The Goddess Ma 'at wrote the tenets to train the Kushite to defend against social Chaos. She believed that there was no better way to fight evil than through the concept of honor.

The Anu-Kushites had already demonstrated that humanity was capable of reaching the God-like state of honor. Kushka and Kushkara proved this with the sacrifice of their own lives for the survival of others, not of kin. The Goddess Ma 'at decided to make each tenet a quest for honor with the ultimate reward of peace.

The courage to pursue honor is made more accessible if you stand for more than just yourself. The real strength of a Kushite warrior lay in his/her selfless determination to see justice for all of God's children. The Kush understood that moral behavior is of more significance and meaningful when done in the name and cause of universal justice.

The Kushite also recognized that words and deeds define the soul. If your words and deeds are consistently honorable, you are living a life of consistent truth. The

Kush called this relationship between word, deed, and consistency, the <u>trilogy-of-truth</u>. The moral consistency of your words and deeds will reveal if you are an Apepa (evil human being) or Kushite (moral human being).

The Ma 'at teaches that honor is not something given to you by others. Greatness is built into your character through the observation and acceptance of right over wrong. Some are born honorable, while others couldn't recognize it if it stood before them in the form of a mountain. Most of us must struggle to find honor. When we find it, we are made whole! The Ma 'at connects personal honor to your ability to control your lesser instincts. With moral behavior as its focus, the purity of the Ma 'at can illuminate your path to spiritual salvation.

The Ma 'at and the Concept of Causality

The Ma 'at encourages the Kushite to believe in the concept of causality. Causality is the belief that there is a spiritual relationship between cause and effect. The idea directs that your actions will have an impact on the universe; rather, you believe this or not. Causality demands that the Kushite act with civility and respect toward others and their property regardless of social status.

The Kushites believed that if you act honorably, it encourages others with honor to serve honorably. However, the Kushites were not naive. The Kush knew that honorable behavior only promotes honorable behavior among those who are fundamentally moral. Note that this has nothing to do with moral perfection. No one is without sin! The Apepa has no morality, and as a result, he/she can never achieve honor.

A short list of Kushite acts of honor from the Ma 'at:

- ◆ Try to keep your word.
- ◆ Apologize when wrong.
- ◆ Always maintain a proper Kushite demeanor.

- Lead by example.
- Respect the property and territory of others.
- Do not insult or humiliate others unless morally deserved.
- Never sabotage anyone or anything unless it's part of a justifiable war.
- Take no action that would lead to a personal loss of integrity.
- Be generous and gracious to others.
- Project a positive and hopeful message to others.
- Try not to destroy those who trust pass against you.
- Do not placate or compromise evil, for this will only help it grow.
- Defend your family honor and the honor of the Kush.
- Accept responsibility when you are wrong.
- Never blame others for something you are responsible for.
- Be respectful to others even when it is difficult to do so. However, you are not obligated to accept anyone's abuse.
- Do not insist on being right when confronted with the beliefs of others.
- Take risk in your professional life.
- Be humble yet proud in your demeanor.
- Be bold in your beliefs.
- Do not argue or debate with those who lack the power to change anything.

The Feather of Justice

One of the most iconic symbols in the Anu-Kushite religion is the single ostrich feather. The ostrich feather is the crown on the head of the Goddess Ma'at. The feather represents justice and is worn upright by the Kushite warrior in times of war, down in a time of peace.

The upright ostrich feather symbolizes a Kushite's just motivation to kill the enemy in the name of justice. It is the immoral and unjust deeds of the enemy that justifies their slaughter. The Kush used this justification to unleash relentless hell upon their enemies in war.

Feather of the Ma'at is the symbol of justice

The ostrich feather is also associated with the Kemet/Kushite burial story. This myth states that a pure heart, the heart of an honorable person, will weigh the same as the feather of justice. The Kushite, with a heart as light as a feather, would be allowed to pass into paradise. If the person is Apepa and has a heavy heart filled with wrongdoing, the heart of that person would be eaten by the Alligator god Ammit. The spirit of the evil person would then descend into everlasting damnation in the underworld.

Kushite Legend of Jebel Barkal

You cannot discuss Kushite religion without mentioning the sacred mountain of Jebel Barkal. While there are other holy mountains in Sudan, Jebel Barkal was iconic to the religion of the Kush.

Sacred Mountain of Jebel Barkal with ruins of the Temple of Amun

Jebel Barkal was believed by the Kush to be the place where all life, including humankind, began. The Kush also believed that the mountain was inhabited by Amun, the supreme God of creation.

Jebel Barkal is located at the third cataract of the Nile river close to a large natural bend. It is upon this mountain that the Kushite Pharaoh Taharqa declared himself the King-of-Kings, ruler of the land of the two cobras, and conqueror of the Libyans.

Today, this mountainous outcrop is a UNESCO world heritage site, and remains the ancient center of Kushite religious life.

Chapter 8 – Kushite Definition of Civilization

How the Kushites Defined Civilization

The Anu are the first people in Africa and perhaps the world to practice agriculture by irrigating the Nile valley, building dams, inventing science, create complex architecture, arts, and writing. Despite these remarkable achievements, the Anu did not believe that these actions defined civilization or greatness.

In the mind of the Anu, mechanical feats could be performed by any of the children of Amun. The Anu also did not believe that it was the intellect, war machine, or physical beauty that made them civilized or superior to others. The Anu felt that it was the cultural acceptance of the principles of the Ma 'at (morality) that made them superior to other human beings. The Kushite code of human decency (Ma 'at) not only defined the Anu people, but it also represented the very meaning of the term civilized.

The Ma 'at was also the moral foundation of the Anu-Kemet and Kushite cultures. The reason is simple, the Anu-Kush and the Anu-Kemet were of the same origin. When forged from a common root, the core of each branch remains the same.

Purpose of the Trilogy-of-Truth

The Apepa (evil or those without morals) will hide from the site of the just. The Apepa will use criticism, religion, blame, politics, false words, and self-serving deeds to conceal the profound wretchedness of their spirit. But the Kush will expose the demon with the ultimate weapon of justice called the Kushite trilogy-of-truth.

Word, Deed, Consistency!

The moral human being will grasp the tang of the Kushite sword of truth, and with it, destroy the minions of Chaos and grind their deceitful spirits into the sand. The sword of truth is a question were the only possible answers are yes or no. Yes, or no represents the purity of truth, which, according to the Kush, has no gray area.

You can wield the sword of truth against any lie, and it will be made transparent. With the trilogy-of-truth, the Kushite warrior will engage the demon Chaos in relentless combat for the hearts and souls of humanity.

The Weapon that Reveals Intent

The Trilogy-of-Truth is a powerful weapon that can be used to expose the intent of any word, act, strategy, or policy. It was the view of the Kush that motive and purpose are different sides of the same coin. A spoken motivation is an alleged reason for an action, while the true intent is the real reason (hidden agenda) showing why a person supports an activity, policy, or strategy.

The morality of words and deeds can be determined by comparing its compliance with the tenets of the Ma 'at. When the Apepa speaks or performs an act, they often try to hide its evil intent while providing socially acceptable motives for their actions or policies. But the Apepa cannot fool the Kushite!

Stated motive alone does not always reveal real intent. You expose purpose by evaluating the rationale behind the policy, its relationship to morality, and its actual effect on others. You can recognize the evil in any justification by using the trilogy of truth as your guide. Look for inconsistencies in the alleged motive and the actual outcome of the act. If reason, alleged purpose, and result are not consistent, then the policy is either flawed or corrupt. In either case, you are witnessing the word and deed of a potential enemy!

Origin of the Word Apepa (evil or immoral)

In circa 1650 BC, the Kemet nation (lower Egypt) was invaded and conquered by the Hyksos. Years after Hyksos rule began, a Hyksos king by the name of Apepi was placed upon the throne of Egypt. Apepi the Hyksos was considered by the Kemet to be vain, cruel, and a ruthless overseer. Among the Anu-Kemet and the Anu-Kush, the name Apepi (Apepa) became synonymous with the concept of evil.

The Dangers of Situational Morality

The Trilogy-of-Truth has an additional purpose within the Ma 'at. It discourages the common social disease the Kushites called situational morality. Situational morality is a moral position that is inconsistently applied to extract advantage or to punish a perceived enemy unfairly.

Situational morality is most obvious in corrupt government, legal and political theaters. An example would be the demand to obey a law that is unequally applied or that the law enforcers do not abide. You'll also note that only a targeted person or group is punished when the law is broken. The clue that most exposes the pathology of situational morality is its inconsistency (hypocrisy).

Situational morality is, by definition, inconsistent and is often worse than having no virtue at all. The problem is that the value is inconsistently applied, creating an enemy of the just. Inconsistency is perceived by humanity as unjust, and this perception will breed conflict and contempt for the law.

Every society claims to be moral and promises to run its affairs based on freedom, justice, blah, blah, blah. The truth is, most governments are corrupt, and the rest are often incompetent. Morality fails to have any real meaning when only applied to give an advantage to others. The Kush felt that the inconsistent application of morality reduced virtue too little more than a cynical excuse.

The Principle of Consistency

Consistency is the third rail in the trilogy-of-truth. The Ma 'at calls consistency the miraculous weapon of truth. The principle of consistency demands balance in all things. If something is out of balance, it is said to be inconsistent and in a state of Chaos. Balance is both the goal and essence of the Ma 'at and if followed, will lead to peace.

If a law is both moral and justly applied, it is (balanced), and deserves the respect of the Kushite (moral human being). If a law is immoral or unjustly applied, it is inconsistent (imbalanced) and must be resisted by the moral. Inconsistency in the application of an otherwise moral law would place that law into a state of imbalance. If a statute, value, law, or tenet is inconsistent, it will become a weapon of Chaos and a source of conflict.

When a Kushite is a witness to injustice, he/she is witnessing a lack of moral consistency. A community without moral consistency will become a breeding ground for conflict, discontent and violence. The tolerance of inconsistency (injustice) enables corruption to flourish, resulting in a disharmonious and despicable society.

Consistency cuts through the confusion promoted by the lies of the minion, exposing their real motivation and strategy. Consistency has a translucent effect on lies enabling you to see right through them.

Propaganda (public lies) are the primary currency of Chaos. Anything that reveals the lie also exposes Chaos. Chaos does not wish exposure for fear of being cast aside. Chaos knows that to look upon its hideous form would lead all but the most wicked to seek its destruction.

The Wretched Gifts of Chaos

The (Apepa) is a living servant of Chaos. Without minions, the strength of Chaos and its negative effect on humanity would be significantly reduced. To prevent this, Chaos bestows several evil gifts upon the minion and promises them the rewards of these sinister gifts. What are these rewards given to the minions of Chaos? Wealth and unlawful power over others! To acquire wealth and power, Chaos encourages amoral values and behavior among his minions. The minions use these satanic virtues as weapons to execute the destructive agenda of Chaos.

The Chaotic Gift of Avarice (**Greed**)

Greed, or Avarice, is the minion of selfishness and insatiability. Avarice is the driver of oppression, violence, unhappiness, and discontent. It enters the mind of humanity and fills it with the hollow promise of happiness and spiritual salvation through ownership. So deceptive is the minion Greed that it hides from its host the futility of the material quest. Greed is a motivating evil that can start at a reasonable level and end with the total consumption of the user's soul.

A ticket to paradise and the favor of a respectable God cannot be purchased with gold. No matter how much an individual may own, in the end, greed will rob you of your immortal soul. If a soul covets wealth in life, everything of worth will be withheld from that soul in death. No Kushite should die rich, having done nothing to relieve poverty and hardship within their realm of possibility and influence.

The Minion Sloth (**Laziness**)

Sloth is the minion of laziness and irresponsibility. The sloth is destructive to the greater society in that this sin encourages and excuses a person from family and social responsibilities. These individuals often turn to crime as a fast and easy path to social status. Every Kushite should engage in work or a business enterprise, and generate a productive, honest living.

Do not confuse the sloth with the man who looks for but cannot find employment. Sometimes those who appear to be sloth are, in reality, your brethren in distress. Your divine empathy (golden gene) will show you the difference. If a person is in trouble, feed them without judgment. While a person in distress deserves support, do not allow empathy or pity to enable the sloth that exists in all of us.

The Minion Pride – (**Narcissism**)

The minion Pride (narcissism or self-love) is the ego in love with itself. The prideful person is a delusional narcissist that believes themselves to be better and more deserving than others. The narcissist believes that they are entitled to special treatment, and consideration rather earned or not. Pride with arrogance is exceptionally divisive and can promote both family and large-scale social conflict. The Anu-Kushite felt that pride with humility is beneficial to humanity when used in these six ways:

1. Pride in your family.

2. Pride in your personal accomplishments.

3. Pride that drives self-improvement.

4. Pride that restrains anti-social behavior.

5. Pride in your contribution to the benefit of others.

6. Pride in your dedication to the principles of decency.

While pride is essential to human progress, it must be tempered by a dedication to human decency. The Ma 'at will help you defeat the adverse effects of pride and assist you in maintaining internal balance. Your internal stability will assist you in maintaining control over those all too human eruptions of envy driven pride. It is essential to understand that where pride drives conflict, there's an abundance of ignorance, insecurity or jealousy driving the pride.

The Minion **Willfully Ignorance**

Ignorance is defined as a lack of knowledge that, in and of itself, is not evil. Evil injects itself into Ignorance by encouraging the individual to ignore facts that conflict with an acquired belief. This type and level of Ignorance is unique and referred to as willful Ignorance.

With willful Ignorance, the person wants to be ignorant to avoid admitting a mistake or as an excuse to side with blatant immorality. The minion willful ignorance actively deprives themselves of any information that contradicts their beliefs. Willful Ignorance seeks like-minded individuals to avoid dissenting opinions and alternative moral views.

Knowledge deprivation enables the willfully ignorant to feel comfortable with their beliefs no matter how ridiculous, sadistic, or immoral. These individuals can create preposterous rationales for their ideas, none of which have a base in common decency. As long as there is a reinforcing source of support for the ignorant opinion, the naive view will persist.

The willfully ignorant is usually the first to shout insults or accusations of guilt towards others. They base their unqualified opinions on feelings with or without the ability to explain or defend their position. The willfully ignorant often knows that their opinion is wrong or immoral and will use hostility and aggression when challenged.

The willfully ignorant cannot offer a moral rationale to justify their position. To do so would be to expose the real motivation, which is often filled with fear, animus, and moral depravity. Even when the willfully ignorant opinion has been debunked, they will not surrender to truth. Don't waste your time trying to change the mind of the willfully ignorant, for this will only lead to their entrenchment and ceaseless attacks.

The Minion Audacious – **The Immoral**

The Audacious minion is a corrupt, immoral, and shameless Apepa who roams the earth without conscience or remorse. This minion is often driven by pride, which feeds into their lack of concern for others. They often have a tendency to seek acceptance of extreme solutions. The Audacious has no humanity and can dazzle you with their brazen and outrageous words and antics. Their tricks can easily be mistaken for competent leadership by the immoral, foolish, and misinformed.

The Audacious is most dangerous in their remarkable ability to influence others to perform harmful acts. Audacious is vulnerable and can be neutralized by exposing their deep-seated immorality. The Audacious always leaves a trail of destruction with blatant attempts to conceal it. You can use their path of evil to track and destroy them. The biggest mistake one can make is to placate the audacious, for this will only make them stronger.

The Minion of Undisciplined **Lust**

Lust like ignorance is not in and of itself evil. This fact makes Lust a real danger to the undisciplined. Beware the minion of Lust because its true purpose is deceit. Lust is designed to trap and control the naïve and leads them onto an unseen path of self-destruction.

There are very few combat strategies more effective than that of the soft embrace of Lust. It will make you vulnerable to all other vices. The minion Lust will lure the carnally undisciplined into a compromising circumstance, rendering them ineffective as a vessel for good.

The minion Lust is divisive and profoundly corrupting. It has a corrosive effect on unity and a destructive impact on social harmony. Undisciplined Lust is quietly corrosive and can destroy both family and nation. Worse yet, the most damaging effects of undisciplined desire is often visited upon the innocent.

The Minion **Envy**

Envy is a horrific minion who also happens to be the underlying reason for many human conflicts. The minion Envy is the catalyst for a thousand other sins, all based on a petty human emotion called coveting. A person who covets can rationalize that they are entitled to something that belongs to someone else. Envy can manifest itself in the form of hatred, greed, prejudice, rivalries, grudges, spite, and malicious intent neatly packaged in a single poison pill. The problem with Envy is not just that it is immoral; it is also highly deceptive.

Envy is a human emotion that can be triggered by events, both good and bad. Jealousy can turn the good fortune of a friend into a divisive rivalry that destroys brotherhood.

Like any other sin, Envy can only enter your heart if you allow it to do so. You'll know when Envy is occurring because it will make you feel hostile toward others for self-serving and irrational reasons. Envy is a normal reaction to the loss of commonality, but it must be immediately vanquished from the moral mind of a Kushite. Resentment will occur because your human, but you must figuratively slap yourself when it does. To the Kushite, Envy is a weakness of character and smells like pettiness. Reject Envy in all of its forms so that it does not pollute your soul and suppress the upward mobility of your tribe.

Recall the old analogy of the crabs in a crowded barrel. When one crab fights its way to the top of the barrel and is just about to escape, a crab of envy will grab his brethren, and pull him down. The Kushite crab will grab his brother by the leg, and with all of his might, give him the final push he needs to escape. The escaped Kushite crab will then turn to his brothers and sisters in the barrel and extend his claw to assist the next in their effort to escape.

There is no place for Envy among the Kush! Those who allow Envy to infect their minds will cause failure, conflict and disunity among the Kush. You must rejoice in the good fortune and accomplishments of others and give them the praise and respect they deserve. The Kushite will take one additional step to combat Envy. That step is to create your own source of achievement so that Envy has no place to grow. The key to defeating Envy is humility. The Kushite wants to see all Kushites succeed because each moral success adds to the greater glory of the Kush.

The Minion **Tribal**

Tribalism is defined as the loyalty one feels for their tribe, affiliation, team, color, faith, or ethnic group. Tribalism has been a useful instinct for the survival of the human species since it began. However, like everything else associated with humanity, tribalism has two distinct sides. The positive side of tribalism enables people to form teams for collective protection and survival. The negative side of tribal convinces the immoral to pursue violent domination and discrimination against the other.

The minion tribal can be petty and indiscriminate. Tribal is capable of taking the most insignificant difference and making that difference into an excuse for war. Tribalism is divisive and will lead humanity on a collision course with itself.

The ancient Kushites knew that it was imperative to establish a strong tribal identity. Without the tribal instinct, I doubt mankind would have survived the paleolithic period of our development. However, the negative side of the minion tribal is its ability to override reason and human decency. Tribalism is as intense a catalyst to conflict as ignorance, and they often work together. Yet the real danger of tribalism lay in its ability to morph into a thousand manifestations of the same sin.

Humans naturally subdivide! Individuals become a family, that becomes a team, that becomes a tribe, that becomes a state, that becomes a nation. When it appears that humanity will enjoy a taste of unity and peace, petty subdivisions within a nation can ignite into a national conflict. There seems to exist within humanity a seemingly insurmountable tribal tendency to forego justice and discriminate against the other. The Kushites referred to this human tendency to subdivide as the Tribal Mask. When we put on our tribal mask, we hide the face of our soul. The tribal mask can act to blind the user to the humanity of others, creating a new reason for conflict.

The divisiveness of tribalism can distort and divide positive concepts like family or faith. No matter what you are, think you are or wish you were, you are in fact identifying with a tribe. Political parties, families, clubs, religion, vocations, and even grade school sports teams are all miniature representations of a tribe. The minion of tribalism knows that each tribal manifestation is an opportunity to sow disunity. The ultimate goal of the minion tribal is to see the entire world at each other's throats. Tribal wants global chaos, destruction, and genocide, driven by humanity's common inability to recognize itself.

The Kush realized that disunity is the primary result of the minion tribalism. This knowledge can be used as a weapon against this beast. You control tribalism's minion by giving the tribe a moral and more expansive reason to exist. To elevate the meaning of tribe, the Kush added the tenets of the Ma 'at. Those who lived by the principles of the Ma 'at were deemed moral and were accepted despite other differences. Those who did not follow the tenets were considered evil and were rejected by the tribe.

While the Kushites attempt to control tribalism was honorable behavior, sometimes even they failed. However, failure is never a reason to stop trying. If we don't try to contain tribalism, it will be the sin that destroys humanity in all of its forms.

Divisive Strategies of Chaos

If you wish to conquer the beast Chaos and its minions, you must first understand their strategies. The primary strategies used by Chaos are the promotion of divisiveness, disunity, and conflict. Chaos and his minions rarely use a single vice to attack. Two or more vices confuses the defender and moves the odds for success in favor of Chaos.

The techniques used by the minions to spread Chaos are varied. These techniques represent every evil (ism) this world has to offer. Examples of these evil ideologies are:

Religious fanaticism
Unrestrained capitalism
Unrestrained communism
Fascism
Racism
Sexism
Totalitarianism
Absolutism
Libertarianism
Know-nothings
Nihilism
Anarchy

All of the isms listed above and many more, have a profound history of failure. Yet, humanity foolishly insists on returning to these failures as solutions to peace. If peace is what you seek for yourself and your nation, the Kushites should be your guide. Drop the isms and turn to and live by the simple universal code of human decency.

Kushites Worship Morality

The insincere shout the name of God while ignoring everything moral the lord God stands for. If your God is truly God, then know that the lord does not seek or require your adulation. For like the Kush, the good lord demands virtue, not worship!

While the Kush certainly worshipped their Gods, they also noted and responded to religion's most significant flaw. A flaw ignored even by today's great faiths. This religious flaw exists in nearly every religion on earth and is the primary reason why faith can no longer solve a single human problem.

Faith's weakness is its relentless focus on worshiping God at the expense of morality and human decency. Yes, the priest and zealots will wag their tongues with moral platitudes while ignoring the immoralities they passively support. When faith becomes more about God, dogma, and wealth than about morality, it no longer holds relevance to the human condition.

Chapter 9: Kushite Art and Architecture

Kushite Origin of Egyptian Architecture

I'm introducing you to Anu-Kushite architecture for the same reason I showed you Anu-Kushite myth, religion, and history. It has been too long that we of African ancestry have passively allowed outsiders to define our history. It is time to aggressively resist the culturally biased opinions of others whose true agenda is to obscure the greatness of the moral Anu. The more you understand about the Anu-Kush, the more you'll realize just how much you have in common with them. This knowledge will enable you to use the wisdom of the Anu in your struggle against Chaos.

The Amelineau (Anu) was the first to occupy the Nile river valley more than 8000 years ago. The Anu is the ancestral origin of all the tribes of south, east and central Africa, including the Kemet (Egyptians). The Anu were the founders of the cities of Esneh, Erment, Qouch, and Heliopolis. These predynastic cities have the characteristic symbols which denote Anu ancestry.

Who Built the Great Pyramid

No architecture in Kemet is more definitive than that of the great pyramid and the sphynx. I agree with modern

Egyptologists who believe that the great pyramid was built by the pharaoh Khufu. In identifying the builder of the great pyramid, Egyptologist has inadvertently proven the Anu (black African) origin of Egyptian architecture. I have already shown you the bust of Menes, the first pharaoh of Egypt. The statue of Menes depicts a man of black African ancestry regardless of the ridiculous theories to the contrary. It is impossible to escape the question, what race was Khufu, the builder of the great pyramid?

Bust of the Pharaoh Khufu

Look upon the face of the Pharaoh Khufu above and try to convince yourself that he is not Anu. As a geneticist, the face above is phenotypically black African, regardless of the angle upon which it is viewed. To deny the historic accomplishments of a tribe because of their race or faith is to discriminate against all of humanity. Please note that I describe Khufu as being phenotypically black African, not stereotypically black African. There can be a world of difference between these two descriptions.

Egyptology is often guilty of believing that black people have a singular stereotypic appearance, but nothing could be further from the truth. Genetics has shown that black Africans possess the highest amount of genetic variation on earth. Black Africans are generally accepted as being the origin of the human race, and their features can be seen throughout the entire spectrum of humankind.

If you have the good fortune to visit the great pyramid at Giza, don't just look at the stones. Allow your imagination to capture the face of its builder. In doing so, you will come to understand the true complexity of those who are simplistically called black. Here is another picture of Khufu to help you visualize the face of the man who ordered the creation of the great pyramid.

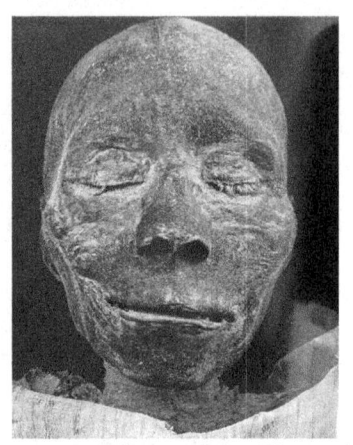

The postmortem face of the Pharaoh Khufu

Sculpture of Khufu's Son Djedefre

Khufu's son, the pharaoh Djedefre is also phenotypically Anu, and his name points to his Anu-Kemet heritage. Khufu and Djedefre were initially given credit for building the Sphynx. However, there is varied and sometimes inconsistent evidence supporting this theory.

The Face of Khafre

Other Egyptologists believe that Khafre built the Sphynx. There is little supportive evidence for this determination. The Sphynx most resembles Khufu. It might be that Djedefre or perhaps Khafre altered the face of the Sphynx from a lion to that of Khufu, their beloved father or grandfather. My personal belief is that the Sphynx was constructed long before Khufu's time and represented the Anu-Kushite God of war Apedemak, the Lion. In fact, the Sphynx may have been built by an Anu King long before Egypt became Egypt.

Face of Khafre son of Djedefre

Ignoring the argument about who built what, the indisputable conclusion is that all of these early pharaohs were Anu-Egyptian. They were also Grandfather and Sons of the same royal and genetic family line.

The Face of Menkaure

The Pharaoh Menkaure also appears to be phenotypically Anu. I would argue that these early pharaohs alone, more than prove my theory of the Anu origin of Egypt and its iconic architecture.

Face of the Pharaoh Menkaure

The People who Built Kemet

The Anu-Egyptians were highly creative, experimental, and prolific builders with unique architectural and artistic styles dating back before recorded time. Many of the architectural styles attributed to the Egyptians is, in fact, Anu, because the Egyptians themselves were Anu. There is no longer any argument that the Anu existed in the Nile delta long before Egypt existed. The original Kings of Egypt were ethnic Anu, as demonstrated by the sculptures of the Pharaoh Menes, Khufu, Djedefre, Khafre, and Menkaure.

Kemet and Kush did later become two separate and unique cultures, but this separation is an entirely different story. Make no mistake about who beget who. Egypt is a product of the Anu, not the other way around. I admit that it can be difficult to tell what is Egyptian and what is Kush when it comes to structural archaeology in Sudan and Egypt. However, I believe that the primary reason for the similarities is that the two civilizations have closely interacted for millennia and have a common origin.

If you dig into Egypt today, you'll undoubtedly find Egyptians of various races, creeds, and colors. Dig deeper into Egypt, and you'll discover its creators, the Anu. Given the common ancestry and close if not identical location of Kemet and Kush, the similarities between the two architectural styles are not at all surprising. Put another way. The Anu-Kush did not copy the Anu-Egyptians because they were the Anu-Egyptians. Likewise, the Anu-Egyptians did not copy the Anu-Kush because they were the Anu-Kush.

Structural Design of Kushite Cities

A straightforward example of early Kushite architecture can be seen in the old city of Kerma in Sudan. Kerma is located within the region of the third cataract known as the northern Dongola reach. Kerma is believed by the Kush to be the city-state of their origin, thus the title Kerma people.

Kerma is known for its dynamic architecture, which shows an exceptionally high degree of urban planning. The city had an extensive harbor facing the Nile. Old Kerma contained structural evidence of homes, palaces, fortifications, storage facilities, government buildings, cemeteries, and more.

The archaeology of Kerma city indicates that the political structure of the kingdom was more complicated than the nondemocratic political system of Egypt. Authority in Kerma was distributed over an expanded class of elites that included royal dignitaries, wealthy merchants, priests, and high officials.

Kushite cities like Kerma, Kurru, Napada and Meroe were well planned. The city streets were stone or gravel and laid in a cross pattern converging onto broad avenues. Buildings were constructed in a variety of sizes and shapes. Homes were built in units with enclosed areas for animals and supplies. Most family housing units were simple dwellings

Old Kerma showing Deffufa in background

surrounded by barrier fences or walls. Kerma city buildings were usually constructed of mud brick, fired brick, wood, or stone. Wood was uncommon in this period, with much of it imported from the south. Scientists believed that the Kerma area was less arid 5000 years ago with rainfall twice that seen today. You would expect to see more palm trees and other subtropical plants in Sudan at that time, along with some adaptive semi-desert vegetation.

Ancient Astrology at Nabta Playa

Nabta Playa is an ancient settlement located in the western desert at the level of the second cataract of the Nile. Nabta Playa is located deep in the western desert very close to the modern Sudanese border. During this time period, this was the land of the Kush. This site is believed to have been used by the ancient Anu. This settlement is believed to have been built around 10,000 B.C. The Nabta settlement is impressive because it once again supports the existence of Anu-Kush during the Neolithic period. More interesting is the finding of what is believed to be an ancient astrological observatory modeled very much like Stone Hinge.

Astrological Stone Cycles at Nabta Playa

Archaeological evidence suggests that this area of the Sahara was much wetter during the Neolithic period. It may have been much more like a savanna with lakes and streams. The Anu living there at that time would have been comfortable enough to begin developing advanced cultural practices like astronomy and mathematics.

The Deffufa Temples

Kushites began building their burial sites near what was known as a Deffufa temple. These large temples were usually located in the heart of the city and were surrounded by graves, homes, shops, storage facilities, palaces, and other buildings. The exact utilization of the Deffufa temples is not fully understood. Legion states that the Deffufa was a combination, astrological observatory, burial chapel, religious temple, and community center.

The Western Deffufa in the old city of Kerma is the largest of the three known deffufa temples. The Western Deffufa had an estimated height of around sixty to eighty feet (20 to 25 meters) with a massive stone foundational footprint.

Ruin of Western Deffufa at old city of Kerma

The Western Deffufa appears to have been a large double flat-roofed temple with multiple floors, levels, towers, and niches. The architectural design of the Deffufa temple is sophisticated and uniquely Kushite. The main Deffufa was surrounded by a multi-building complex that encompassed an area of several hundred acres. What I'm about to mention is purely speculative and coincidental. However, my training as a 3D animator made the structural shape of the Defuffa impossible for me to ignore this coincidence.

The basic shape of the Deffufa appears to be remarkably like that of the secret mountain of Jebel Barkal when viewed from the side. Could it be that the form of the Deffufa temples are purposefully derived from the shape of this mountain? If so, then the Deffufa was also a temple to the God Amun.

Mount Jebel Barkal

Compare the two pictures on the prior page. The front portion of the Deffufa ruin could represent the uraeus (cobra on crown) of the pharaoh. If so, this finding demonstrates a relationship with the God Amun and the sacred mountain of Jebel Barkal at the earliest period in Kushite history. This architectural possibility so ignited my interest that I decided to reconstruct in 3D how an ancient Deffufa temple would have appeared. (Next page).

My 3D Reconstruction of the Western Deffufa

I have never visited the western Deffufa, so my 3D reproduction had to depend on existing photos of the building. The main steps leading to the top of the Western Deffufa shown below start at the base of the building complex and lead to a rooftop observatory.

Ruins of the Western Deffufa Today

This stair design replicates the stairway that once led to a small temple on the top of Jebel Barkal. The rooftop temple contained a large open area with a small alter believed used for astronomy or religious ceremonies. Please see pictures of my 3D reproductions of the western deffufa on the next few pages.

Western Deffufa Side View

The above is a full side shot of my 3D reconstruction of the Western Deffufa as it would have looked thousands of years ago. The rooftop stairway is located in the right-hand corner of the building. I created these reproductions in full color. Unfortunately, my book is in black and white.

Western Deffufa Stairway to Rooftop Observatory

The New Ma'at

Rooftop Observatory of the Western Deffufa

Frontal shot of Western Deffufa as it appears today

Above is a frontal snapshot of the ruins of the western Deffufa as it exists today. The above structure has an uncanny resemblance to the gates of the Egyptian hyper-hall style temples. This structure is constructed of fired brick and stone, which explains the uneven weathering of its surfaces. The next picture represents how this frontal view would have looked thousands of years ago.

Frontal shot reproduction of Western Deffufa

Opposite Side shot of Western Deffufa

Back side reproduction of Western Deffufa

The Kushite Speos Temple

Another of the oldest temple types created by the Kush is called the Speos Temple. A Speos temple is usually formed by expanding an existing cave or crack in a rock surface of a Cliff.

Reproduction of a Speos Temple at Jebel Barkal

Speos temples were common among the Kemet and the Kush and used for the worship of many gods. There is evidence of Speos style temples at Jebel Barkal and other sacred Anu-Kushite religious sites dated before the existence of Egypt.

Speos Temple at Jebel Barkal

The primary characteristic of the Speos temple is that they are built into cliffs and contain a cave-like inner sanctum. The exterior portion of these temples can vary greatly, but they are all cave temple sanctuaries. The most famous of the Speos style temples is the Temple of Abu Simbel. The Pharaoh Ramses II built this Speos temple. Essentially, Abu Simbel is an elaborate Speos temple built into a sandstone cliff. The interior of Abu Simbel contains a narrow chamber leading to a small chapel.

Temple of Abu Simbel

This temple was originally located near the shore of the Nile. It had to be relocated to higher ground as a result of the Aswan dam project.

Facial sculpture of Ramsas II

Standard Kushite Dwellings

The dwellings of ordinary people were usually made from mud brick. These traditional dwellings could be round or square. The small round hut structures often had a single entrance, one or two windows, and a roof made of reed or papyrus. At one time or another, every human on earth once lived in a house like this.

Reproduction of Kushite Mud Hut Homes

The square Kushite dwellings were also typical. Some were singular, and some contain multiple attached rooms or segments of various sizes, centered around an enclosed courtyard. The exterior of the mud brick hunt was made smooth with plaster and was often painted in vivid colors.

Reproduction of Kushite fired mud brick home

The square Kushite dwellings were also typical in Egypt. Varied quality of brick was used in the construction of a Kushite home, while public structures used fired brick or stone. The Kushites often used a combination of brick and stone, which explains the uneven erosion seen with many ancient Kushite temples. Kushites built different styles at different times in their history. Some styles evolved into newer, more elaborate designs while other styles were abandoned entirely.

Architecture During Napata Period 900 BC to 270 BC

Egyptologists often ask, why did the Kush build pyramids long after the Egyptians had stopped? The answer is obvious! Egypt stopped building pyramids because of the expense, outside cultural influence, and a gradual cultural disconnect from the original pyramid builders. The Anu-Kemet/Kushite were the original pyramid builders, and the Kush continued to relate to the old culture of the Anu.

The Kushites often returned to the old ways in areas they controlled. In the early Napatan period, royal Kushite burial structures began to transition from the low angle pyramids to the acute angle pyramid. These acute angle pyramids were usually three to forty meters in height and made of fired brick and/or stone.

Wide angle Kushite pyramids at Napata

The burial pit of the low angle Kushite pyramid was located under the pyramid structure. In some tombs, these low angle pyramids had elaborate entrances that lead to a three-room chamber that held the sarcophagus. Altars or shines were built in the front of the pyramid, as was the custom of the Anu-Kushite and the Anu-Egyptians.

Royal Kushite wide Angle pyramid at El-Kurru

Below is a 3D reproduction of a wide-angle Kushite pyramid design. I've left open the burial pit of our low angle pyramid, enabling you to get a better idea of how these buildings were constructed. There would also be a long stairway with side walls leading down to the burial chamber.

Reproduction of open low angle Kushite tomb

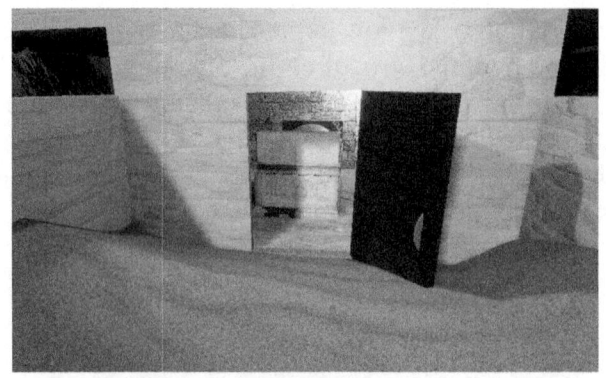

View inside crypt of wide-angle pyramid burial pit

View inside royal wide-angle pyramid crypt

View from inside wide-angle pyramid crypt

Temple of Amun at Jebel Barkal

Jebel Barkal is one of the oldest and most important archaeological sites on the African continent. Located just below the bend of the third cataract of the Nile river, Jebel Barkal was the spiritual center of the Kushite religious universe.

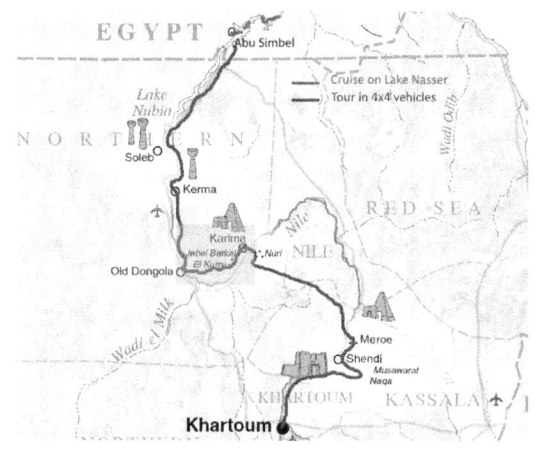

Map showing location of Jebel Barkal

Jebel Barkal is a small mountain outcrop or yar-dang that is believed by the Kushites to be the location upon which the God Amun stood when he created humankind. Over millennia, Kushites have built multiple temples to their Gods at Jebel Barkal, none of which was more revered than the God Amun.

Jebel Barkal with ruins of the temple of Amun

The Temple of Amun at Jebel Barkal was designed in what Egyptologists call the hyper-hall style. This style is prevalent among Egyptian temples and is claimed by most to be of Egyptian origin.

I believe that the Anu is the origin of this temple style simply because their earliest temples showed most of the common characteristics that define the hyper-hall style. Here is my reproduction of a typical Kushite hyper-hall temple:

Kushite Amun Hyper-hall Temple

The hyper-hall style varies but almost always contains a massive doubled based pylon front gate with a central rectangular or arched entrance. Massive columns, statues, or Stella usually adorned the entrances. The hyper-hall style is essentially a series of open rooms filled with large Columns.

Some rooms were enclosed while others were open, containing massively decorated columns making up the bulk of the structure. These temples were used for various religious ceremonies associated with the God Amun.

Kushite Hyper-hall Temple of Amun

Regardless of the origin of the temple style, there is no doubt whose God was being worshiped. The God Amun has been the supreme God of the Anu-Kushite since the birth of the Anu faith. A series of Anu-Kemet pharaohs built the largest of the Amun temples at Thebes. However, Pharaonic addition, the practice of laying claim to a previous ruler's work, acted to obscure the true origin of these temples.

Kushite Temple of Amun side view

The El-Kurru area near Jebel Barkal contains numerous temples to various gods. Most of the temples are in poor condition, with a few in partial reconstruction. Here are a few reproductions of Kushite architecture:

Temple Library at the foot of Jebel Barkal

Reproduction of a Goddess Shrine at El-Kurru

Reproduction of a Goddess Shrine at El-Kurru

Architecture in Meroitic Period 270 BC to 400 AD.

There are many different locations, types, and sizes of Anu-Kushite architecture that exist from the second cataract of the Nile to the ancient city of Meroe. Anu-Kushite architecture changed over time, giving us several manifestations of their work.

Dendera Style Kushite Column

The Dendera column style shown above are exclusively Anu-Kushite and were used for structural support, political propaganda, and declarations of leadership. The Dendera column is named for the location upon which these columns were found. The Dendera temple lies to the north of Luxor on the west bank, not far from the second cataract of the Nile.

Some of the most iconic of the Anu-Kushite designs occurred during the Napata and Meroitic periods. One of the most famous is the iconic Anu-Kushite pyramids. More than 240 of these distinctive pyramids were built within the kingdom of Kush over the millennia.

These acute -angle Kushite pyramids were not built just for the Royals. Many elite Kushites built pyramid temples for their family members ranging in size from a few meters to more than seventy meters in height.

Meroitic Kushite Acute Angle Pyramid

The design of the acute angle Kushite pyramid usually included a debris-filled inner core with an outer core made of stone or fired brick. The pyramid's external structure was covered by a smooth plaster and decorated in brilliant colors. The Kushite pyramids had a sharp angular configuration when compared to the older Anu-Egyptian style.

Both Anu-Egyptian and Anu-Kushite pyramids contained a capstone. The Kushite pyramids capstone was rumored to include a vault holding the treasures of the buried individual. This rumor, which proved to be inaccurate, was the driving force behind the destruction of many of these fabulous pyramids by foreign treasure hunters.

Kushite Pyramid Capstone

While there were several historical incidences where an invader would enter the land of the Kush and destroy things,

these infiltrators never lasted long. Most of the damage to
the Kushite pyramids began after the introduction of Islam
in the 6th century A.D. The Islamic leader Mohammad Ali
was said to have had a vision that instructed him to destroy
all of the pyramids of the Anu-Egyptians and the Anu-Kush.

Ali's advisers whispered the possibility that blowing up
monuments might damage the foundations of the city of
Cairo. Ali wisely chose not to take this action, saving these
structures for posterity. Ali's real intent was to destroy all
symbols of the old religion because it acted as a continuing
threat to his Islamic faith. Despite this, the world should be
grateful for this historical stroke of good luck.

The number of Kushite pyramids also help to assure that the
Kushite would not be forgotten. There were reportedly more
than 250 Kushites pyramids in Sudan. There are less than 100
pyramids discovered in all of Egypt.

Destruction Came from the West

Notably, in the 1800's AD, an Italian named Giuseppe Ferlini
entered the land of the Kush for the sole purpose of finding
treasure. This buffoon discovered and destroyed the tomb of
Candice Amanishakheto (Amani-Shakheto). This great female
regent initiated the creation of the Meroitic script.

Giuseppe Ferlini also destroyed the capstones and structures of
many Kushite pyramids in an attempt to find treasure. This
destruction was totally unnecessary because most treasures
were believed to be buried beneath the pyramids per Anu-
Kushite tradition. It is only in the most recent decades that the
government of Sudan has been capable of protecting Kushite
monuments, preserving what is literally the ancient legacy of
black Africans in the entire region.

Kushite Royal Palaces

Kushite royal residences varied in size and styles. Many of the most brilliant palaces are located in the cities of El-Kurru, Nuri, Napata, and Meroe. These lavish palaces typically housed royal families, high ranking officials, and a significant military unit.

Reproduction of a Kushite Palace

Kushite palace aerial view

Aerial view of Kushite palace boat dock on the Nile

Kushite Fortifications

In the year 1878 BC, the Pharaoh Senusret III ascended to the throne of Egypt. During the latter part of his reign, he and the Egyptian kingdom came under significant financial stress. Senusret's solution to this problem was to attack the northern region of Kush and rob them of their wealth. As with any surprise attack on a peaceful neighbor, Senusret enjoyed limited success against the Kush. His goal was to steal Kushite gold to support his failing leadership.

Like so much of Egyptian and Kushite history, the Senusret III episode has been completely distorted by a Eurocentric interpretation of the historical evidence. The Egyptologist believe that Senusret III defeated the Kush and expanded his control deep into Kush territory. Senusret III is also given credit for building a series of "intimidating" fortresses to keep the Kush at bay and "under control" (dominated). Once again, the Eurocentric Egyptologists have projected their cultural bias into the history of a people they fail to understand. In this segment, I'm going to explain why the Egyptologists are at best half-right and, at worse, continue to perpetuate warn-out cultural stereotypes.

Senusret Claims Victory

The pharaoh Senusret III created a stela claiming victory over the Kush. Here is what Senusret claimed:

I have made my boundary further than south than my father.
I have added to what was bequeathed to me.
I am a King who speaks and acts.
What my heart plans is done by my arm.
One who attacks to conquer and swift to succeed.
In whose heart a plan does not slumber.
Considerate to clients, steady in mercy.
Merciless to the foe who attacks me.
One who attacks him who would attack.
Who stops when one stops.
To stop when attacked is to make bold the foe's heart.
Attack is valor, retreat is cowardice.

Since the Kush listens to the word of mouth, to answer him is to make him retreat.
Attack him, he will turn back.
Retreat and he will start attacking.
They are not people one respects.
They are wretches, craven hearted.
My majesty has seen it, it is not untruth.
I have captured their women.
I have carried off their subjects.
Went to their well and killed their cattle.
Cut down their grain and set it to fire.
As my father lives for me, I speak the truth.
It is no boost that comes from my mouth.

The above Senusret stela is little more than a coward's manifesto. He executed a surprise attack upon the peaceful Kushite with an attempt to detract his people from his failure of leadership and to improve his perceived status. However, history shows that his deceitful aggression against the Kush was both short-sighted and short-lived.

The True Story of Senusret III

Egyptologist insists that a series of forts were built on the Kushite territory by Senusret III, whose twelve-year reign ended 1878 BC, the same year the above stela was created. This essentially means that Senusret would not have had time to build the forts that are credited to him.

Please also note that Fort Buhen and Semna are less than one-hundred-fifty miles apart. This would make Senusret's so-called invasion of Kush little more than an incursion. In between these two forts is the major Kushite goldmine of Wadi Halfa. The goldmines are a clear indication of Senusret's true motive for the sneak attack upon the Kush.

Kushites Built these Forts

I believe that Egyptians did not build these fortifications for several reasons. It is far more logical to assume that the Kush built these forts years before the reign of Senusret III or his father. The Kush built these forts because the Kush had to protect their livelihood as gold merchants. Please note that all of these forts are built well within in Kushite territory. The forts are built along the Nile highway implying that they might have been used for storage and transport centers for valuable Kushite goods.

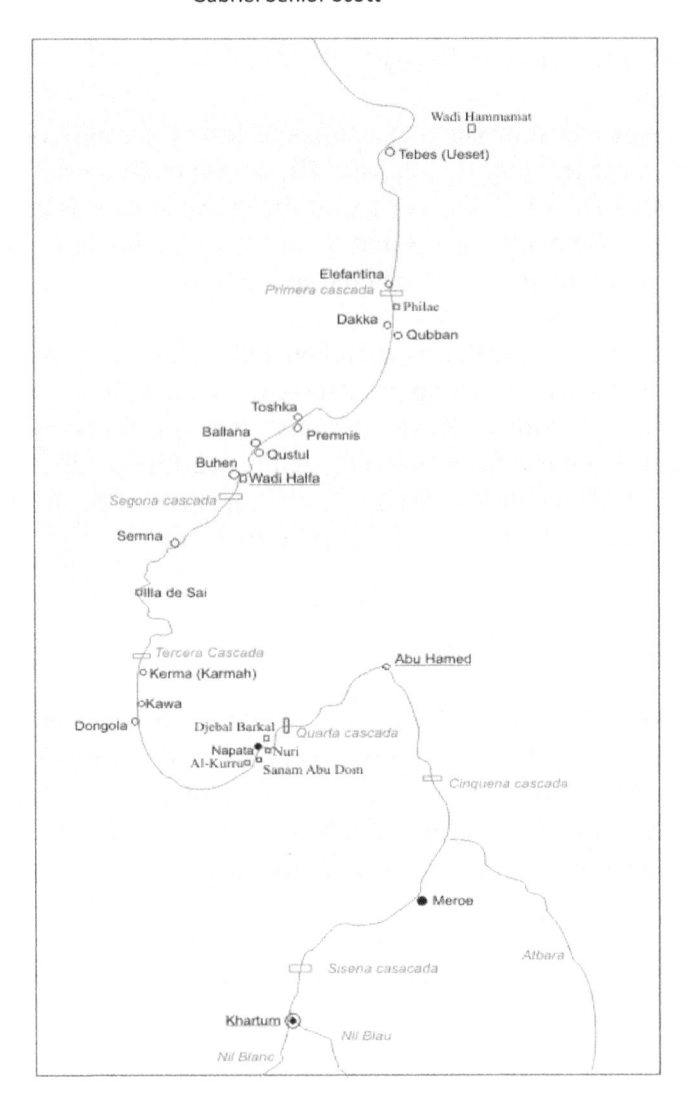

The largest forts built at Buhen and Semna are very close to the main Kushite goldmines. It would make good sense for the merchant Kushite to build fortifications as a safe harbor for valuable products such as gold and as secure trading post. This also explains the large number of forts spread deep into Kushite territory. The number and location of these forts makes sense because products were being transported north from deep within the African continent.

Design of these Kushite Forts

The design of these forts is also a strong clue to who built them. While Kushite and Egyptian architecture is similar, there were some important differences. Let's take a closer look at the largest of the forts located at Buhen.

The Kushite Merchant Trading Fort at Buhen

The Kushite fort of Buhen is massive, covering an area ten times larger than a few football fields. Such an enormous fort is not practical if built purely for defense. Yes, the fort was surrounded by massive walls, but the walls were not made of stone. The basic design of the fort was common to Kushite construction. The fort contained a stone outline or base. The protective walls some forty to fifty feet high were made of thick fired brick reinforced by large timber beams. Several of the wood species used at Buhen was imported from interior Africa. The Egyptians acquired their timber in trade with the Kush, so it is doubtful Egyptians would have used this expensive material in a fort design.

Note also the layout of the Buhen fort. The defensive lines or ramparts are designed for archers of which the Kush were renown. The massive interior spaces are not practical and would be tough to defend against a regular army. This leads me to believe that housing an occupying Egyptian force was not Buhen's purpose. If the walls were breached, the enemy would be immediately at your doorstep with only archers to defend the interior fort. Buhen is not a practical design for a combat fort.

Buhen also has three main entrances, one by land and two on the Nile side. The two Nile gates make the fort more venerable to attack but more efficient for offloading massive amounts of valuable goods. Note also that the two entrances on the Nile side lead directly into the enter sanctum of the fort. This interior space contained large, closely packed storage areas, offices, and barracks nearly impossible to defend. The storage areas were massive and held far more grain and materials than would ever be needed by its three to five hundred defenders. Buhen was a massively fortified storage facility and trading post, not a fort designed to intimidate the Kushites as some Egyptologists have suggested.

The Kushites were Primarily Merchants

Note also the large open spaces from the land side of the Buhen fort walls. These broad areas would be perfect for an open marketplace for commercial trade, but terribly hard to defend against a formal military force. The fort's design makes sense only as a means of protecting valuable goods stored in the interior fort as deals are made in the open marketplace areas.

The landside entryway also makes no sense as a purely defensive structure. The gate is large and bifurcated, making it easier to control the flow of people entering and exiting the fort. However, the gate is poorly designed for keeping out a trained military force. Everything about Fort Buhen points to a massive Kushite trading post were gold, and other valuable goods were traded.

Sorry Egyptologist, but the notion that the enormous Kushite fortress of Buhen, and all the other Kushite fortresses built along the Nile, were used to intimidate or control the Kush is ridiculous. It makes far more sense to assume that these forts were constructed by Kushites, on Kushite land to protect Kushite commercial trade.

Occupied by the Kush

Kushites, not the Egyptians, occupied the Buhen, Semna and all the other fortresses in Kushite territory. The fortresses were surrounded by Kushite villages, deep within Kushite lands. If Buhen and other forts were created to keep out or harass the local Kushites, again, the forts are poorly design for this purpose.

It is also important to reiterate that none of the Kushite forts appear to have ever been attacked. I find it hard to believe that the Kush would have allowed the Militarily weaker Egyptians to occupy their lands and steal their gold without a fight. These silly notions about the Kush do not square with the nature or history of the great Kush. In upcoming chapters, I will detail the military superiority of the Kush and show you how the notion of them being dominated by any outside force is biased fantasy!

The Pharaoh Senusret III

There is one final fact that leads me to believe that the Pharaoh Senusret lied when he claimed in his stela to have defeated the Kush. That final fact is Senusret's image shown above. Note that he <u>does not</u> wear the double uraeus symbol representing Kingship over the lands of the two cobras. This pharaoh appears to have been little more than a brazen opportunist, liar, and a thief!

Chapter 10: Just Wars of the Kushite

Kushite Wars Explain Kemet Origin

Few other events can better explain the origin, development, and character of a nation than its wars. The Anu-Kush were exceptional warriors, and in the next several chapters, you'll learn just how successful their war machine proved to be. The Anu-Kush did battle with the most powerful military forces that existed in the ancient world. More often than not, the Kushites proved themselves the victor.

Despite the importance of these issues, the Anu-Kushite's combat prowess did not come from their weapons, training, technology, or tactics. The Kushites acknowledged that every human being is afraid to die! The Kush believed that there was no shame in fear of death unless it froze your ability to fight for justice. The Kushite also knew that courage is a spiritual force that resides within a person's values and is enhanced by their training.

To the Kush, the two most important tenets that guide your behavior in wars were the concept of self-possession and the principle of courage. The Kush believed that the acceptance of these two Ma'at doctrines would wipe the fear of death from the equation of war, making you an unbeatable opponent.

The Concept of Self-Possession

Self-possession is defined as an intense need to preserve self and community. It is a tribal reflex that exist in all of us. Self-possession is a state of internal calm, confidence, and control that comes when a person is in a state of inner harmony. The self-possessed understand themselves. They accept and acknowledge their imperfections and use this humility to make better decisions. For the Kushite, self-possession was as fundamental to the development of a warrior as weapons training. Self-possession represents a warrior's inner strength. Self-possession demands that the warrior be self-reliant, self-sustaining, and self-defined. Depending on others for these markers of valor would be considered cowardice by the Kush.

Kushite symbol for self-possession

Self-possession speaks to the importance of having confidence in one's moral values. Self-confidence is built by knowledge, preparation, and sacrifice. Your values enable you to recognize when a fight is worth your life even when faced with overpowering odds. But what makes self-possession work is knowing what you're fighting for is moral. The morality of a cause will enable the morally prepared to sacrifice for the greater good.

Self-possession provides the strength you need to overcome fear and move your moral agenda forward. There are spiritual powers and an almost arrogant disregard for safety that comes from believing that you are morally correct. If you combine these feelings with the balance of the Ma'at, (how you treat others), it will place you on a righteous path to victory even if you die in the process.

People who are not self-possessed are vulnerable to the immoral persuasions of others and have an out sized need to be accepted by the Apepa. They tend to become willing victims of criminals, cults, charlatans, political, and religious predators.

The minions of evil can smell the unpossessed person and will use this weakness against them.

The warrior who is not self-possessed will be tormented by unreasonable fear. They will exhibit a type of concern known as risk anxiety or risk aversion. This type of fear makes it difficult for a person to bear the emotional weight of taking on a potentially life-changing opportunity.

Outsized fear among the Kush was considered a contagious disease. The Kush believed that if you allow fear to fester among the people, it will infect the entire society. The Kushite knew that where fear reigns, tyranny is not far behind. The Kush also felt that the key to defeating fear lay in the individual's commitment to a higher purpose that turns fear into determination.

The warrior who has mastered the moral tenets will, by nature, performed extraordinary acts of courage in the name of morality. These individuals are rare and are known as the Supreme Kushite Warrior. To hold this title is the ultimate goal of every devoted Kushite!

By embracing the concept of self-possession, you will achieve your purpose by sheer force of will. Self-possession enables the humility, courage, and fortitude required to stand alone in the face of overwhelming odds. When a Kushite sees a supreme (moral) warrior, respect urges him/her to emulate the warrior, knowing that they are in the presence of greatness!

Self-possession also encourages creativity, collaboration, social progress, and an aggressive need to assimilate others to the way of the Kush. In today's valueless world, you'll need to start with the strength of character and profound courage inherent in the virtue of self-possession. Here is an example of two supreme Kushite warriors:

Colin Kaepernick, Eric Reid

> These young warriors are the ultimate example of Kushite self-possession and courage. These two Anu-Kushites stood alone in the name of justice and did so when faced with overwhelming odds. Their reason for action is the continuing genocide against African Americans by the American injustice system. They demonstrated the deep Kushite conviction that evil is evil no matter what form it takes. Anthems, flags, and phony patriotism will not hide the immoral acts of animus that pollute the soul of this nation. While there are tens of thousands of such heroes, these two young men stand forever as a public testament of what it means to be a Supreme Kushite Warrior.

The Tenet Courage

In the war against Chaos, the warrior needs to be courageous to the point of self-destruction. The strength of a warrior's courage can be measured by their devotion to a code of human decency. This level of courage can only come from a dedication to a higher moral standard. A moral standard that elevates the warrior beyond self is the key to its effectiveness.

Kushite symbol for Courage

The most devoted of the Kushite warrior class is called the Ta-Sety (Bowman, Sniper, or Assassin). In ancient times, the Ta-Sety personality type was encouraged to become a military commander or a priest because both were considered equally dangerous!

These individuals tend to have rigid personalities and struggle with the meaning of the tenets. While the Ta-Sety loves the Ma'at, they are volatile by nature. The Ta-Sety will stand their ground and can become pathologically focused on the completion of a mission. The Kush primarily used them in times of war for assassination and sabotage.

The Ta-Sety has no fear because, in their minds, fear is replaced by anger. Fear and anger cannot exist at the same time. The lack of fear within the Ta-Sety is rooted in the Kushite pronouncement, which is a declaration of self. It is said that where the Ta-Sety stands their ground, it is the same ground the enemy will meet their demise.

The Ultimate Courage of the Female

In ancient times, there was a forty-five percent chance that a mother would not survive her pregnancy. And yet, women still bore their children with courage and without complaint. They also, in their survival, were laden with the additional responsibility of motherhood and upholding the cultural essence of their tribe. This fact was true then, and it is still true today!

The female Kushite also fought side-by-side with the male similar to that of the Israeli army today. Every Kushite male and female were required to learn the skills of the Ta-Sety (bow, sword, wrestling, and horsemanship). When a Kushite warrior stood before his/her enemy in preparation for combat, leadership reminded the young warriors of <u>female courage</u>.

"If she can endure the risk of bearing your child, the site of your enemy should not raise a single bead of sweat upon the brow of a Kushite warrior."

The Pronouncement

Among the elite of the Kush, there was a formal ceremony called the (Pronouncement). During this ceremony, the warrior publicly declares that they are Kushite and dedicated to the way of the Kush.

I am Kush because it is what I choose to be!

This tradition was carried forward by King Kushta, father of the Great Pharaoh Piankhi. King Kushta made it a daily practice to declare his dedication to the Kush. His words would carry throughout the kingdom, inspiring his people to greatness. "I am Kush," said the great King Kushta, "and so are you!"

When young men and women stand for justice, as did Colin and Eric, they are making a profound moral pronouncement that will be heard for centuries to come. In their heroic action, these men have declared themselves noble. They have also unknowingly, declared themselves Kush, a moral human being!

Glorification of Nonsense

Kushites referred to wars fought for economic advantage or domination as the wars of the parasites. Driven by the minion greed, the objective of these amoral conflicts was to rob others and prosper from their toil. Parasitic wars are started by the Apepa (evil minions) and suffered by all. The Kushites believed that the only acceptable reasons for war were in defense of life, land, and justice.

The Kushite also felt that parasitic wars were the glorification of nonsense and a curse upon humanity. The civilizations that are the most parasitic are also the least moral and harmonious. If the wealth and power of a society are derived from parasitic violence, then violence is the God they worship. A parasitic culture will eventually implode as a result of injustice and internal conflict. Those who profited most from parasitic wars will abandon their supporters and those who risked their lives to win these immoral endeavors.

The International Kushite

The Kushites performed extensive trade with distant lands. The ancient Kush knew about the world, and the world knew about the Kush. The societies of the outer regions, as the Kush referred to them, had long heard the rumors of Kushite wealth. These foreign societies developed an irrational lust for Kushite gold and would attempt to take it. This perverted lust for Kushite wealth is the origin of the word Nubian, referring to the people of gold.

Sometime after the Anu-Egyptian became independent, a few of its leaders foolishly attempted to take what belonged to the Kush. Then over the centuries, so did the rest of the known world. The Kush did battle and defeated the greatest military-based empires on this planet. And yet, not a whisper of their victories can be found in western history.

To truly understand the Kush and the importance of black Africans in history, you must know why the Kushites went to war. You will discover that every Kushite conflict reflected their devotion to justice and the code of human decency.

Ancient Kushite Weapons of War

Among the Kushites, the knife, mace and ax are the earliest weapons used in combat. These tools naturally evolved from the daily chores of working people.

Ancient Kushite weapons of war

The mace was also used as a symbol of royal power and was created in several sophisticated designs.

Kushite hand carved wooden mace

The spear was also a standard Kushite weapon for thousands of years. One of the oldest of the ancient tools, a spear's length, and tip underwent numerous modifications in adaptation to hunting, fishing, and war.

Depending upon the enemy, the Kushites developed several different weapon tips and arrowheads. There were stone, copper, and iron spear tips found at various archaeological sites. Combat spears were also customized by length for differing combat situations.

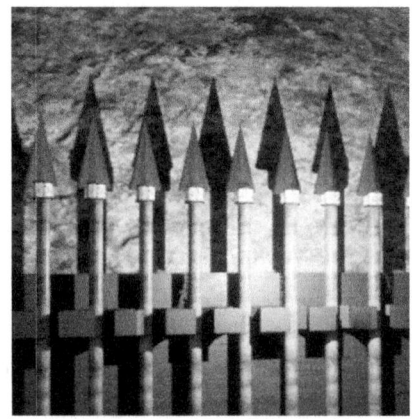

Kushite Combat Long Spear

The Kushite shield was another of those weapons that evolved with the quality of the enemy. The first shields and body armorer of the Kush were made of animal skins, textiles or woven reeds. These materials would only protect from the most primitive of weapons. When more sophisticated civilizations threatened the Kush, reeds proved to be insufficient. The interactions with other cultures forced the Kush to update their shields to iron.

Kushite Textile Family Identification Shields

To the Kush, the shield was more than just a defensive weapon. The combat shield was also used by the Anu-Kush to identify a tribe, individual fighting units, and even rank. The most used markings for the various contributing tribes were the textile and animal skin patterns.

Very much like a bird would represent an American state, the Kush used the zebra, leopard, lion, elephant, giraffe, and textile patterns to represent supportive tribes within the Kingdom. Reed gave way to the animal skin, which gave way to wood, which gave way to metals as the enemies of the Kush themselves grew in military sophistication.

Iron was introduced in direct response to foreign invaders, some of whom used metal weapons and shields. The round iron shield with the central disk became a trademark of the Kushite warrior.

Kushite warrior with metal combat shield

While the short digger was used early in Kushite warfare, the long sword was adopted as a result of foreign conflict. Kushite swords, daggers, and even arrowheads were designed for a particular purpose. Weapon tip technology evolved from stone to Abyssinian, copper, and on to iron.

Ancient Kushite Weapons

The Kushite Bowman

Of all the Kushite weapons, none were revered more than the bow. Every child of the Kush, male and female, was required to become Ta-Sety (Assassins of-the-bow). Mastering the bow is the skill referred to by the Kush as the "eye-of-the-fly". The bow is mastered only when the Bowman can metaphorically shoot an arrow into the eye of a moving fly. The skill of the Kushite bowman was part of the myth of Kushite invincibility portray to the outside world.

The legends say that the Kushite warrior in battle were vicious and relentless. They had a propensity for shooting arrows into the eyes of the enemy. Attacking the eyes was both practical and a deliberate tactic to instill fear and hesitation in the hearts of the enemy. The eye-of-the-fly technique induced significant reluctance on the part of potential invaders.

The Bowman was the sniper of the ancient world, and the Kushites were the masters of this skill. The bow was used in various ingenious ways by the Kushites on the battlefield. However, it was the accuracy and exceptional range of the Kushite bowman that sealed the fate of their enemies.

The original Kushite bow was the renown long-bow used by every civilization on earth. The basic design of the longbow provided the power and accuracy needed in field combat.

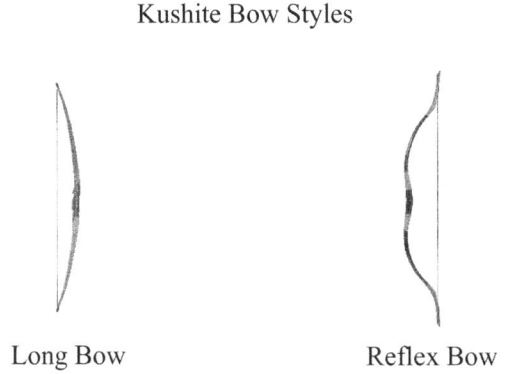

Kushite Bow Styles

Long Bow   Reflex Bow

The Kushites incorporated the smaller reflex bow into their arsenal shortly after the Hyksos invasion of northern Egypt. The reflex bow was easier to manipulate when fighting from a chariot, elephant, or horse.

The Kushite Warrior and the Horse

The horse was an essential and revered part of the Kushite culture. While oxen and donkey were used for the transportation of goods, the horse appears to have lived a noble life. Among the Kush, the horse was used for transport, recreation, commerce, and war. The horse was the most beloved animal in the land of the Kush, and riding skills were as essential as that of the bow. Horses were also a social status symbol, and most importantly, a weapon of war. The Kushite Kings kept large stables of horses and encouraged horsemanship throughout the kingdom.

Museum representation of a Kushite war horse

While the chariot may have been introduced to the Kush by the Hyksos, the horse was not. The horse was introduced to the Kush by a tribe known as the Punt. The Punt was an Anu-Kushite tribe located in the south-eastern horn of Africa. The Punt was known for their agricultural abundance and horsemanship. The Punt was peacefully assimilated by the Kush, bringing with them their remarkable horsemanship. The Kush incorporated the horse into their cavalry, field messaging and scouting.

Kushite Warrior and the Elephant

The Kushites were known to trade in elephants originating from central and southeastern Africa. The Kush established a trading settlement on the island of Abu at the second cataract of the Nile as early as the 4th millennium B.C. The term Abu was used to describe the sacred elephant.

The Greek translation of the word Abu was the word elephant, and the island of Abu came to be known by the Greek term Elephantine. From Elephantine, the Kush controlled the commodities trade from the African interior. One of those commodities, of course, was the Abu.

Statue of ancient Kushite Elephant Cavalrymen

I can imagine a time in Kushite history when the Carthaginian Hannibal Barca, visited the bustling markets of Abu (Elephantine) in search of combat elephants. I can envision Hannibal inspecting these massive and intelligent Abu for health, strength, and aggression. The noise of commerce and the strained voices of haggling merchants rose from the dusty markets as Hannibal made quiet preparation for his war with the Roman.

The Kush used the Abu as a strike force weapon against military field formations. The elephant cavalry struck fear in the hearts of the enemy and complimented other field formations like the horse cavalry, chariot brigades, infantry, and archer.

The infantry was subdivided into various weapon specialties such as the swordsmen, axmen, spear and archer units. This approach to the military organization was so compelling that the Kush rarely suffered defeat in battle. While many invaders defeated the Kemet (Egyptians), those same invaders never defeated the Kush.

Kushite Warrior and the Chariot

Egyptologist claims that the Hyksos introduced the chariot to Egypt and subsequently to the Kush. Maybe! The chariot is often mentioned as the technology that enabled the Hyksos to defeat the Egyptians. If this is so, why didn't this same technology conquer the Kush?

In many modern texts written about the Kush, you're going to find ridiculous conclusions about their status and intellectual capabilities. Ignore these references because they are culturally biased. Their goal is not to enlighten the world about the history of the Kush, but to perpetuate stereotypes. Having said this, let's examine the possible origins of the combat chariot in the lands of Kemet and Kush.

Ancient Kushite horsemen and chariot riders

Some historical accounts led us to believe that the Kush got the idea of the chariot from the Hyksos or the Assyrians. How could this be true when neither the Hyksos nor the Assyrians had horses of native origin. Egyptians and Kushite Stella indicate that the Hyksos and the Assyrians got their horses from the Kushite tribe known as the Punt. These exchanges were made primarily through Kushite trade or as gifts to the royal families.

The Assyrians spoke extensively about the Kush and their remarkable expertise with the horse. But where did the chariot concept come from? Could it be possible that a people who were expert horsemen and used donkeys to pull carts, might one day replace a donkey with a horse to invent the chariot miraculously? I'll leave this cynical question for you to ponder.

Kushite Warriors and the Ostrich Feather

In many depictions of the Kushite warrior, they are shown wearing a single feather in their hair. The Kushite warrior is known as the warrior of the Ma'at, or the warrior of justice. The most iconic symbol of the Goddess Ma'at is her simple crown of golden ribbon and a single ostrich feather in her hair. The feather represents peace, harmony, and justice. The Kushite warrior would only wear the ostrich feather in the upright position in battle. The feather represents the correlation between the Ma'at and the just cause of the war.

Kushite warriors in battle

When Kushites go to war, the feather represents the moral justification for the coming carnage to the enemy.

Kushite Antidote for Fear

The Kushite antidote to fear is righteous anger. The human being cannot feel both fear and anger at the same time. One must give way to the other. If you know your cause is moral as defined by the Ma'at, your fear will transform into just-anger and a resolve to see, justice fulfilled, even at the cost of your own life. Once the transition is made from fear too righteous anger, no force on this earth can stand against you.

Your enemies count on fear to control you. If there is no fear, the enemy has no leverage upon which to manipulate. The only other option your enemies have is brutal aggression. As you would in the ancient Kushite tradition of wrestling, use the weight of your enemy's aggression to skillfully counter their moves. As the enemy attacks, they are unwittingly recruiting more Kushites to the cause. If the enemy uses violence, you are free to use force to resist. Be creative, relentless, and ruthless in your attacks. If the enemy is stronger, use irregular warfare. Hit hard, hit deep! Attack the den of your enemy to demonstrate your disrespect for their strength, which will unnerve their cowardly strategy of violence.

War Reflects Moral Character

The Kushite wars described in the next few chapters demonstrate the moral character of this remarkable tribe. Guided by the Ma'at, the Kushites were aggressive people who did not shy away from war. The Kush actively sought, practiced, and developed military technology and used it to destroy their enemies. You must do the same!

Despite what the Egyptologists say, the Kushites were the dominant military force during most of their history. Regardless of their strength, the Kush only attacked others when threatened. Kushites believed that war should be a last resort and usually reserved it for self-defense. The Kush did not commit genocide, permanently enslave inhabitants, murder children, or actively attempt to erase the history of others. In the enlightened mind of a Kushite, these kinds of barbaric acts would be considered immoral and uncivilized.

Chapter 11: Kushite Wars of the Homeland

A Future of Greatness and Disharmony

As early as 6000 B.C., the area that is today's Egypt and Sudan had already been occupied for millennia by a people called the Amelineau (Anu). The Anu was the black African ancestors of both the Egyptians and the Kush. Many, if not most of the cultural precursors defined today as being Egyptian, had its origin in the Anu. But as you and I know, when it comes to humanity, nothing lasts forever.

Upon the birth of Kemet (3150 B.C.), the Anu-Kush had already existed for thousands of years in this region. The cultural center for these people was located in the Dongola Reach in southern Sudan. From 3150 to 1650 BC, a period of 1500 years, Kemet and the Kush lived in relative cultural harmony. This period of peace was possible because both nations were ethnically and spiritually cohesive.

I would argue that the spiritual cohesion of the Anu-Kemet and the Anu-Kush was the critical factor in their ability to sustain social harmony. When people allow themselves to be guided by a singular definition of justice, all other differences fall by the wayside.

Then Came the Hyksos

Hyksos is a word meaning rulers from a foreign land. This group invaded Egypt around 1650 BC. Its war machine managed to overtake and subdue the independent Egyptian, laying the foundation for about one hundred years of foreign occupation and domination.

I'm not interested in judging if the Hyksos were good or bad rulers. Since they lasted for one hundred years, they must have been more than adequate. However, the Hyksos were not Anu-Egyptian or Anu-Kush. They did not follow the Ma 'at, and I'm sure they gave preference (unequal justice) to their people over the native Egyptians. The Hyksos injected both foreign ideas and ethnic diversity into what had previously been a spiritually homogenous population.

The Hyksos population was centered in the northern delta region of Egypt. The defeated Anu-Egyptian hierarchy relocated to middle Egypt and used this area as their base of operation against Hyksos rule. But what of the Anu-Kush who were not conquered by the Hyksos? I would argue that the Anu-Kush continued with their ancestral tradition of consistent justice and human decency despite the Hyksos.

Slow but Profound Change

The Kemet in the north were experiencing a profound change in how they viewed the world. I would argue that the Hyksos injected just as much good into the body of the Egyptians as they did bad. The negative influence of the Hyksos stemmed from the parasitic invasion. Negative influence also occurred because the Hyksos failed to accept the justice driven principles of the Ma 'at.

By 1550 B.C., the Anu-Egyptian leadership in the south turned to their ancestral bothers the Kush and asked for their assistance in dislodging the Hyksos. These efforts were led by Ahmose I, the first pharaoh of the eighteenth dynasty. The great Kush heeded the Egyptian call, and together, the Hyksos were pushed from power.

The Kushite tribe most responsible for the defeat of the Hyksos was called the Magi. With combat assistance from the Magi, the Egyptians rebelled against Hyksos rule and expelled their leadership from Egypt. This action restored the hegemony of the Egyptian line under the control of Ahmose I.

Peace and Anu-Kemet control over the north was restored, and Ahmose I sat upon the throne of Egypt. However, Egypt already showed signs of cultural change as a result of foreign influence. During the reign of Amenhotep I, son of Ahmosis I, tensions began to rise between Egypt and its brother to the south, the Kush.

Second Egyptian War of Independence

Upon the death of Amenhotep I, Thutmose I came to power. Thutmose I, one of the early mixed-race pharaohs, had a new vision for himself and Egypt. I would argue that Thutmose was the first of the ancient Pharaohs to minimize the importance of the code of human decency. Thutmose I was influenced by the Hyksos and was determined to see a new stronger Egypt rise from the sands of the desert.

Thutmose wanted greater power, so he turned against his own ancestors, the Kush. He decided to push south into Kushite territory to establish the old border that reached to the city of Aswan. In doing so, he found himself in conflict with the Anu-Kush that would set the stage for all future disputes between the Egyptians and the Kushite.

The Pharaoh Thutmose I carried out damaging military raids deep into the heart of Kushite territory. These actions ignited the Princes of Kush into war, and they began a series of territorial retaliations against the Kemet.

Success by Failure

While Thutmose eventually achieved his territorial ambition, he failed to defeat or acquired long-term dominance over the land of the Kush. Even in Tombos, a settlement established by Thutmose was governed by Kushite princes. At this time in history, most of the Egyptian government, military, and priesthood were under the control of the Anu-Egyptians. Thutmose I could not dominate the Kush because Egypt was in so many ways, still Kush.

You might be wondering how the Egyptians might have materially changed from the Kush during and after these conflicts with Thutmose. The changes that occurred between the two cultures took many hundreds of years. From the standpoint of the Kush, the rift was about a moral divide caused by a Thutmose inspired deviation from the code of human decency. The Kush also felt that the behavior of the Egyptian was slowly being corrupted by foreign influence. To the Kush, this meant that the Egyptians were moving away from the tenets of the Ma 'at.

An example of Egyptian behavior that would never be accepted by the Kush was the destruction of an ancestor's public legacy. The practice of destroying a predecessors' monuments and inscriptions was becoming commonplace among the post-Hyksos Egyptians. While Thutmose did not use this divisive practice, several future pharaohs would. These future pharaohs would routinely erase or claim credit for their predecessor's accomplishments to acquire more magnificent glorification of themselves.

The Kushite insisted that erasing an ancestor's legacy would defile the very meaning of the word family. The Kushites also disapproved of the post-Hyksos pharaoh's willingness to dabble in the parasitic business of slavery. Slavery was an abomination to the Kush and was never an accepted part of their civilization.

Hyksos Influence on Egypt

After one hundred years of occupation in the land of Egypt, the Hyksos became intergraded into Egyptian culture. This bicultural integration was especially true in the north. The Hyksos accepted much, but not all, of the Anu-Egyptian beliefs. The critical divergence in this Hyksos cultural marriage was in the concept of justice as defined by the Ma 'at.

The Ma 'at was secondary to the Hyksos. However, the Ma 'at remained vibrant among the Anu-Egyptian people. It would be the post-Hyksos Egyptian leadership in their quest for power who would choose to further weaken the influence of the Ma 'at. The aggressive actions of Thutmose against the Kush would set the stage for all future conflicts between Egypt and the Kush.

I have already discussed the first Egyptian Kushite conflict led by Menes that created the Kemet nation. I would describe the Thutmose conflict as the second Egyptian war of independence from the Kush. Unlike the first Egyptian war of independence, this second war was the beginning of a slow but permanent division of the two civilizations. While the evidence supports that post-Hyksos Egyptians and Kush lived a significant portion of their histories in peace, there were ever increasing periods of conflict between the two nations.

History is Never Simple

After the separation from the Kush, the Egyptians suffered far more external invasions than did the Kush. These invasions dramatically changed the Egyptian character leading to the perceived distinctions between the two Cobra cultures.

Kushite wars were not limited to the Egyptian tribe. As the Kushite and Egyptian empires grew in size and wealth, their borders became the unrelenting target of small Bedouin tribes. These tribes would raid Egyptian and Kushite border settlements for food, water, and weapons. I believe it was the constant border threats that drove the militarization of both cultures. In time, the Anu-Kushite created such a formidable military force that its very existence threatened Egypt.

Several of these small Bedouin tribes were beneficial and were assimilated into the Kush, while others remained elusive. These smaller tribes were valuable to the Kush as a source of military alliances, brides, livestock, weapons, natural materials, and unique skills.

Chapter 12: A Continuation of the Cultural Rift

Hostile Divergence of Egypt and the Kush

Nearly one hundred years have passed since the reign of Thutmose I, who had begun another cultural rift between Egypt and the Kush. During this period, the offspring of Thutmose continued their efforts to expand the power and territory of Egypt. Unfortunately, their efforts to expand were at the expense of the Kush, which further divided the land of the two cobras.

From the pharaoh Thutmose II who ruled circa 1492 BC throw Thutmose IV circa 1390 BC, Egypt enjoyed one its most significant periods of social success and economic power. Egypt built a formidable military force and no longer felt the need to depend upon a Kushite alliance. During this one-hundred-year period, no outside force could threaten the power and majesty of the Kemet.

Amun's Creative Intent Comes True

You may recall the Kushite origin story I provided earlier in this text. I mentioned the God Amun's declaration that the female was created to rule the world, while the male was created to protect her rule. There are only four notable Egyptian queens that have held the power of regent. The first of these female pharaohs was Nitocris, who ruled circa 2175 BC.

The second female pharaoh was Sobekneferu, who reigned after the death of Amenemhat IV. The third known female Egyptian pharaoh was Twosret, the last ruler of the nineteenth dynasty that ended circa 1190 BC.

In Egypt, circa 1479, Amun's intent comes to fruition with the unlikely rise of Hatshepsut, the incredibly competent female Pharaoh of Egypt. Hatshepsut is the most notable of the female pharaohs. Hatshepsut ruled jointly with both her husband Thutmose II and her nephew Thutmose III. To the betterment of Egypt, Hatshepsut was the dominating factor in both these relationships and portrayed herself as the pharaoh of Kemet. She was responsible for the construction of many iconic monuments, including her famous mortuary temple at Deir el-Bahari.

The importance of Hatshepsut to the success of the Kemet at this time cannot be overstated. She was one of the most successful leaders of the ancient world. Hatshepsut, by official ranking, was the queen mother who fed the people of Egypt. She is famous for her exploration into the land of the Punt (land of the gods) to reestablish peace and trade with the Kush. While trade with the Punt had been occurring since the time of Khufu, this relationship broke down with the aggressive actions taken by her predecessor Thutmose I.

One of Hatshepsut's little-known and underrated achievements was the successful transplanting of trees acquired in a trade with the Punt. Sadly, her importance was undermined by Thutmose III, who attempted to wipe her from Egyptian history. Thutmose III also resumed hostilities with the Kush by attempting aggressive and unsuccessful expansion.

During the reign of Hatshepsut, there may have been another authoritative female regent ruling in the Kushite kingdom of Kerma. The Kushite kingdom of Kerma was located just south of Egypt. The Kerma Kush was equal to if not greater than Egypt and existed from circa 2500 BC to 1400 BC. By this point in time, the Kerma Kingdom had evolved into the Kushite empire.

Kerma was also the nation that prevented Egypt from making any significant incursions into Kushite land beyond the second cataract of the Nile. The regent queen of Kerma at the time of Hatshepsut may have been Kandake (Candice) Nedjeh, queen of the Kerma Kush. She was believed to have ruled Kerma circa 1500 – 1460 BC. Both these female leaders were enormously successful and proved the value of Amun's intent to see females as the rightful rulers of the world.

The Vision of Thutmose IV

Thutmose IV is the starring character in the legion of the sphynx. The legend states that Thutmose IV, one of several children of Amenhotep II, was not the most promising in the royal line. While walking in the desert, Thutmose IV came upon the half-buried head of the sphynx. He sat in front of the sphynx and fell asleep. During his slumber, he dreamed that the sphynx spoke to him. The sphynx asked the young prince to free the statue from the sand. If he accomplished this deed, the sphynx promised Thutmose IV that he would become pharaoh. Thutmose IV freed the sphynx from the sand, and as promised, he was crowned pharaoh of Egypt.

Thutmose IV served well and brought prosperity to the Egyptian people. He wisely abandoned aggression against the Kush and, through marriage, reinstated the Anu-Egyptians to full power. He was the father of Amenhotep III, who is the pharaoh that would come to be known as the (magnificent king).

Amenhotep III, the Magnificent King Circa 1390 BC

Amenhotep III was beloved by both the Kemet and the Kush. His status among these two groups enabled him to reign with great prosperity for both nations without the need of war. The Kemet called him Kemet, while the Kushites called him Kush. Amenhotep III was the first pharaoh to peacefully reunited the land of the two cobras. Unfortunately for Kemet, Amenhotep III was the father of Akhenaten, the prince who would become the heretic pharaoh.

Akhenaten the Heretic of Amun

The pharaoh Akhenaten, circa (1355 BC), had a profound effect upon both the Kemet and the Kush. This man attempted to erase the creator god of the Kush and replace him with the sun god Aten or Ra. Both the Egyptians and the Kush resisted this decree, trying to make the pharaoh understand that Amun is Ra. But Akhenaten did not hear or heed the words of the people.

The priesthood of both the Kemet and the Kush was thrown into turmoil by the actions of Akhenaten. To establish the new god Ra, Akhenaten ordered the building of a new city capital call Amarna. He met with resistance from the people and turned to cruelty as a means to accomplish his goal. In Amarna, it is written that vast quantities of food were sat in the open, allowing the god Ra to absorb their goodness. As these foods rotted, the people who built and serviced the city of Amarna starved.

Egypt Returns to Moral Female Rule

In the later years of Akhenaten's reign, he became ill and feeble-minded. To stave off chaos, he awarded a young lady named Merytaten the rank of King's Daughter. This rank, which is the same among the Kush, gave Merytaten the power to control many Egyptian government affairs in place of the King. She was given this position because of her humility and great strength of character. It was said that Merytaten possessed the morality of the goddess Ma'at and the intellect of the royal scribes

The Great Wife Merytaten

Merytaten is believed to be the daughter of Akhenaten and Nefertiti. There is no evidence that Nefertiti in her position as the Queen-mother ever took serious part in government affairs. However, Merytaten held several royal titles and was named the Great Kings wife by the Pharaoh Smenkhkare. The rank of Great Kings Wife was extremely powerful, giving the holder the power to rule in place of the King. Merytaten may well have been the fifth unnamed female pharaoh of Egypt.

Importance of the Female Royal Titles

Since the time of the Anu-Kush, before the existence of Kemet, females were exercising great national power. A female's position was designated by titles such as the King's Mother, the King's Sister, the King's Daughter, the King's Wife, and the Great King's Wife. The two most potent of these titles were the Great King's Wife and the King's Mother. The holder on one of these two titles often acted as coregents within both Kushite and Kemet society.

These titles were not automatically assigned because a person was the wife or daughter of the King. These titles had to be bestowed upon the female for her to exercise its power. This tradition, these titles, and the way they were used are identical among the Kushites and the Kemet. I would argue that this is another piece of circumstantial evidence pointing to a common origin of the two kingdoms.

Kushite Kemet Conflicts Fluctuated

Conflicts between the Kemet and the Kush slowed considerably during the reign of Tutankhamun. Tutankhamun had no heirs and was followed by Ay, an adviser to Tutankhamun. After the short reign of Ay came the commoner Egyptian general named Horemheb. It was Horemheb who destroyed the last remnants of Akhenaten's heresy and returned Amun to his place as the senior god of the Kemet.

Horemheb also had no heirs and was succeeded by Ramesses I. Seti replaced the pharaoh Ramesses. However, it was under the Pharaoh Ramesses II that conflicts between the Kush and Kemet reignited. Ramesses II was also facing military pressure from a growing array of foreign enemies. He wanted to prove himself to be a great warrior King. But his actual military success is highly suspect.

While Ramesses was a great builder and propagandist, I would disrupt his success as a warrior. For example, he was stopped in his tracks when fighting both the Hittites and the Kushites. He was able to raid deeply into Kushite territory but could not hold the territory for any significant period. Ramesses II was dependent upon the Kushite tribes to support his army, yet his propaganda implies that he defeated and dominated the Kush. Both of these social circumstances cannot be true.

The Decline of Kemet

After the pharaoh Ramesses II, Kemet began a steady decline in power due to immorality, internal conflicts, and natural disasters. However, disputes between the Kush and the Kemet had slowed considerably.

By the reign of Ramesses III, the Ma 'at no longer played a significant role in the behavior of Kemet. The Kemet were plagued by corruption and social disorder. During this same period, the Kushites held to the principles of the Ma 'at and were growing in power. For the next four hundred years, Kemet experienced inept leadership and violent power grabs. Kemet faced an evolving leadership vacuum that confused and weakened the authority of the state.

Kemet also underwent a splitting of the nation's power base. There were often two competing pharaohs, northern and southern, trying to dominate the other. These internal struggles further weakened the fabric of Kemet society and compromised their traditional beliefs.

Kemet began to see wealth and power rather than the well-being of its citizens as the baseline for success. The Kemet emphasis on self-gratification induced crime, social injustice, royal infighting, and chaos. While Kemet appeared superficially wealthy on the surface during this period, it was rotting from the inside out.

After this turmoil, peace with Kemet would last for the next seven hundred years, enabling the Kush to tend to their affairs. During this period, the Kush created a vibrant and prosperous nation from Aswan to lands beyond the Blue Nile.

Chapter 13: The Kushite Conquest of Egypt

The Age of the Anu-Kushite Pharaohs

By 745 B.C., what was once the great nation of Kerma had long evolved into the even greater state of Kush. Among the Kush, the code of human decency remained vibrant, allowing peace to prevail within its borders. Meanwhile, kemet was experiencing continuing internal strife that was weakening the fabric of the state. These conflicts were causing disruptions in trade and violent outbursts among the people. This disruptive Egyptian behavior was becoming an existential threat to the Kush.

The Kush had become the supreme military force in the region as Kemet occupied itself with rebellions, Bedouin border clashes, and a chronic failure to control the various tribes of the Levant.

The Kushites exercised power from their kingship in the cities of Napata, Kerma, and Meroe in Sudan. These locations provided a modest buffer from the chaos of Egypt. At this time in history, the Kush was ruled by a mighty King named Meriamun-Piankhi (King Pi), son of King Kushta. King Piankhi was beloved by his people and considered himself a humble Ta-Sety warrior.

King Pi was described as a quiet, introspective man who was a pious follower of the Ma 'at and the old Kushite mindset. While administratively competent, King Piankhi showed little interest in the trappings of power. He considered Egypt's political turmoil to be a threat to the harmony of the Kush. The King ordered all Kushite forces, including the Magi in the northeast, to prepare for war against Kemet.

Multiple Claims to the Thrown

During the Egyptian period from 795 – 744 BC, there were multiple claims to the throne of Kemet from both native Egyptians and Libyan settlers. The tensions that led to the Kushite war with Kemet began some years earlier. In 750 B.C. in lower Egypt, the land above the first cataract was in political disarray. A migratory group called the Libyan from the western desert increasingly dominated parts of Egypt.

The Libyans are said to have peacefully entered Egypt via migration and commerce beginning around 1200 B.C. The Libyans began to compete for local power with the Kemet, causing cultural friction that further weakened the state. Various cities in Egypt were controlled by Libyans, whose leaders started to call themselves pharaoh.

Evidence suggests that up to eleven Libyan governors, with the support of the Libyan nation, conspired to lay claim to the throne of Kemet. This action was problematic for the Kushites. The Libyans did not follow the teachings of the Ma 'at and had no birthright to rule Egypt. It was also rumored that the Libyans wanted to replace Amun as the primary God of the Kemet.

King Piankhi of the Kush lost patience with the political foolishness of both the Kemet and the Libyans. He decided to invade Egypt and take control. The Kushite King's goal was nothing less than the complete reunification of the land of the two cobras, as defined by the ancient Anu.

The Unifying Vision of King Piankhi

The Kushite version of a united- kingdom would mean the complete control of upper and lower Egypt and all the lands of the Kush combined. King Piankhi saw the old Kingdom as a time when Kemet and the Kush were one in peaceful coexistence. The Kushites referred to this united land as the Kingdom of the Two Cobras.

This United Kingdom of the Cobras is represented by the double uraeus crown earned and worn only by the Pharaoh Amenhotep III and the subsequent Kushite Pharaohs. While many Egyptian Pharaohs tried to reunite the lands of the two cobras, only Amenhotep III succeeded until the great King Piankhi. The singular accomplishment of reuniting the lands of the two cobras by force made King Piankhi one of the greatest Kushite Pharaohs who had ever lived, second only to the magnificent Pharaoh Amenhotep III.

The Pharaoh Piankhi wearing the double Cobra Crown of the United Kingdom of Kush.

Retaking control of Egypt, even with the distraction of political turmoil, would not be an easy task for the Kush.

The most crucial battle would occur at the Kemet stronghold located in the imperial city of Memphis.

King Pi also identified the Libyan governors who had attempted to take control of Egypt. Piankhi would especially seek the heads of Osorkon and his brother Takelot who were the governors of Memphis. Takelot was the primary target of Piankhi's rath because he claimed to be the Pharaoh of Egypt. The great King foresaw that nothing less than the conquest of Kemet and the destruction of Libya would ensure a lasting peace. The Egyptian and Libyan armies were in a standoff against each other, both attempting to gain control of the realm.

As was the tradition of the Kush, King Piankhi gave warning to both the Libyans and the Egyptians to stand down. In their combined arrogance, both ignored the demands of the King. Piankhi ordered the Kush to move against the antagonist and confiscate their lands and treasures. He also ordered that the people of both Egypt and Libya be absorbed into the Kingdom of Kush.

The Pharaoh Piankhi's Victory Stella

"I ordered the great Kush forward against it! Mount the walls and penetrate the houses across the river. Thus, Memphis was taken by a flood of water. Multitudes were slain therein or brought as living captives to his Majesty King Pianhi."

The Kushite War of Kemet

King Piankhi ordered his Kushite army to march north and destroy the Egyptian forces standing against him. The King's forces also trapped and destroyed the Libyan army in the field. The warrior king Piankhi then conquered Hermopolis killing a significant portion of the resisting Libyan garrison.

The Kushite King marched to the city of Memphis were the Libyan governor Osorkon and his brother Takelot had prepared to make their stand. The King's army that approached the city of Memphis was so massive that the ground trembled as they approached the city from three sides.

King Pi slowed his army's advance on the city to time the siege to within six weeks of the annual floods. King Pi knew that Memphis was vulnerable to the Nile's annual flood and that it could be used as both a diversion and as a weapon.

Old Memphis sat just west of the Nile in a natural bend that slowed the stream of the Nile as it flowed past the city. Water rises quickly in this space, placing great pressure on the city walls built along the banks. Piankhi recalled from his childhood the damp streets of Memphis during the yearly floods and was determined to use this natural event as a weapon against the defenders. The King and his generals carefully evaluated the topography of the city and created an ingenious plan.

He ordered his men to surround and harass the city, except the side facing the Nile. The King knew that on the Nile side, the walls were designed to protect the town from flooding, but not against a direct attack. The ramparts on the Nile side were lightly defended as the ground it faced was too soft for an army to advance. The King concluded that the wall's ability to hold back water could be undermined by sabotaging its foundation.

While King Pi's forces kept the city occupants distracted with minor attacks, he ordered a group of engineers to remove their weapons and dress as farmworkers. Some of the men performed this common task by day, while others dug narrow channels beneath the city walls by night.

The Kush on the riverside were being watched, but the Libyans saw no threat. The Libyan defenders of Memphis knew that there was not enough space between the wall and the riverbank to place a significant number of warriors, which put their minds at ease. The river's narrow beach was also wet, rocky, and slippery. The mud was deep and would slow an attacker, making them easy targets for the Libyan archers.

As the Kushite engineers worked beneath the wall, workers quietly displaced its stone foundations forming deep crevices. The Kush used metal hammers wrapped in cotton cloth to subdue both the sound and vibration of the strikes. The steady sabotage of the city wall lasted for weeks until the Nile began to rise.

Battle of Memphis

As the floods began, Piankhi ordered a massive attack against the front and sidewall ramparts of the city. These attacks were so fierce that the defenders were forced to move an ever-greater number of defenders to these locations.

As the mighty Nile rose, the waters began to undermine the foundation of the city wall. The walls started to fail, and copious amounts of water flowed into the city, completely inundating it within a matter of days. The streets of Memphis were flooded with water, mud, leeches, snakes, and debris, making the defense of the city all but impossible.

The defenders of the city were forced to move men, weapons, and provisions to higher levels as the siege continued. Animals within the town were running wild, and people were in a complete panic. When King Piankhi's

The New Ma'at

generals determined that the breach was successful, a full siege of the city began.

The main gate of Memphis was quickly breached, and the Kushite army poured into the city, killing all opposition. The battle of Memphis was brutal and destroyed the bulk of the remaining Libyan and Egyptian forces. The King executed Takelot and captured Osorkon during this great battle solidifying King Pi's absolute rule over Kemet.

The King's forces occupied Memphis while a segment of his army moved northwest to conquer Libya. King Pi quickly consolidated his forces and marched on the Libyan nation-destroying all who opposed him.

As you might expect from a moral Kushite King of this magnitude, the Pharaoh Pi having killed his brother, offered the surviving Libyan Governor Osorkon redemption. The King's terms were simple. Surrender your authority to the Kush, and your heart to the Ma'at, and I will give you your life. The King attended to the needs of the defeated. He graciously assured that all were fed, and none were abused.

Osorkon wisely agreed to the terms of the Pharoah Piankhi and was given a place of limited power near Sani. These remarkable acts of mercy by King Pi would prove to be a useful gesture that would later serve the Kushites well. Piankhi's acts of kindness forged his reputation as a strong yet merciful leader that ended all resistance, restored order, and made him much appreciated among those he defeated.

The Redemption of "Osorkon the Forgiven"

Several years after the conquest of Kemet, the Assyrians attacked the Kushites near the city of Sani. Osorkon was given command of Sani as a secret test of his loyalty to the king. It was the Kushite forces under the command of "Osorkon the Forgiven" that drove the Assyrian army from the lands of the Kush.

Upon hearing this, the Pharaoh embraced Osorkon for his loyalty to human decency and declared him a Supreme

Kushite Warrior. Osorkon was declared a man of honor, and a prince among the Kush. The Kushite Pharaoh Piankhi had not just defeated the national enemies of the Ma'at, he also created a Kushite warrior in the person of Osorkon. The gracious Pharaoh Piankhi went on to create the 25th Dynasty of Egypt, which restored peace and prosperity to the people of Kemet.

The Pharaoh Piankhi's Pyramid today at El-Kurru

It is said that the Pharaoh Piankhi quietly returned to his palaces at Napata and Meroe and ruled his empire from Sudan. He installed his sister as the priestess of the cult of Amun and introduced competent administrators in all levels of government. He also restored many temples and reaffirmed Amun as the primary God of the land of the two cobras.

The Pharaoh Piankhi, King of the Two Cobras, was buried in a tomb beneath his pyramid, as was the tradition of the Anu- Kushite. He was laid to rest in the ancient royal cemetery at El-Kurru, Sudan. The Kushite Pharaoh Piankhi attained complete control over the Kingdom of the Two Cobras beginning 740 B.C. He would rule the two cobras for another twenty years before his death.

Chap 14: Kushite Guardians of the Levant

The Kushite Saviors of Jerusalem

The Pharaoh Piankhi the Great, was succeeded by his brother, the Pharaoh Shabako. With the choice of Shabako as Pharaoh, the Kushites once again showed their propensity for choosing exceptional leadership with remarkable moral and national vision.

Kushite Pharaoh Shabako

In the time of the Pharaoh Shabako, the Kushites were in a period of massive commercial expansion. The Kush under Shabako added absolute control over an area known as the Levant. This area is known today as the Middle East. The Levant would include the nations of Jordan, Palestine, Israel, Lebanon, and Syria to the western edges of Turkey.

Under the leadership of the Pharaoh Shabako, the Levant became a protectorate of the Kush, whose forces were needed to repel the Assyrians and other menacing enemies. The Assyrian tribe was growing in strength and threatening the entire region. The nations of the Levant paid tribute to Shabako to protect their lands from Assyrian attacks.

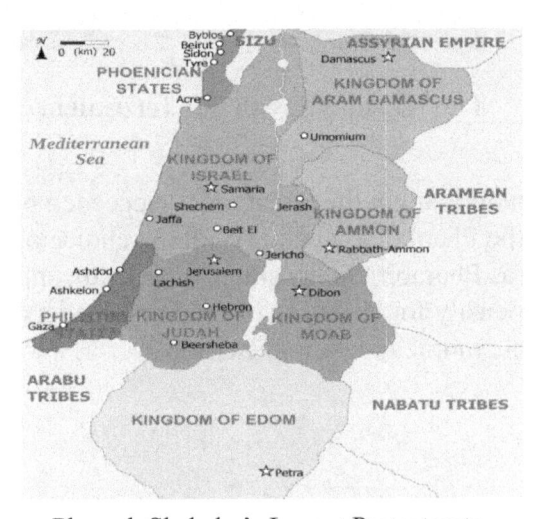

Pharaoh Shabako's Levant Protectorate

The above is a map of the ancient Levant circa 720 B.C. Shabako came to power at a time of modest unrest. A faction within Egypt was rebelling against the Kush. The uprising was subdued just in time for Shabako to begin dealing with the Assyrian problem.

The nations within the Kushite protectorate were coming under threat by the Assyrian army. When the Kushites went to the aid of the Levant, their actions ignited years of conflict with the Assyrian empire. For the most part, the Assyrians were held at bay, but Kushite control of the

Levant was weakening due to constant conflict. Shebiktu, the son of Shabako, succeeded his father as the Pharaoh of the two cobras in the year 702 B.C.

The Kushite Pharaoh Shebiktu

Shebiktu continued the Kushite's fierce resistance to the advancements of the Assyrians. However, some of the nations of the protectorate decided to placate the Assyrians and were quickly over run. There was a massive military encounter between the Kushites and the Assyrians in the city of Tyre. The Kushite forces repelled the Assyrians and saved the city from destruction.

Eventually, the Assyrians took control of the Levant with the exception of those territories directly under the protection of the Kush. The areas that remained with the Kush were Judah, Israel, and the Gaza.

Taharqa, Savior of Jerusalem

There existed among the Kush, a young general by the name of Khuinefertemre Taharqa. This aggressive young general forged his reputation for winning great battles against the Assyrians. This warrior quickly rose to the rank of Field Marshal of the Kush and was nick-named Taharqa the Conqueror.

Taharqa was not a member of the Kushite royal family. He solidified his reputation as an outstanding warrior at the battle of Jerusalem. The historical account states that

Taharqa faced and defeated a much larger Assyrian force and saved the city of Jerusalem from destruction. Among the Israelites, this victory over the Assyrians earned Taharqa the title, the savior of Jerusalem.

The battle of Jerusalem and many other victories lead by Taharqa, sent the Assyrians into retreat. Taharqa's victories also enabled the Kushites to reassert economic control over the Levant.

Kushite Warrior Pharaoh Taharqa

In 679 B.C., the Assyrian King Esarhaddon occupied the state of Judea. He fortified his army and marched into Egyptian territory with the intent to conquer the Kush. He was met by the Kushite Taharqa, who by this time had been crowned Pharaoh of the two kingdoms. Historical records indicate that there was a brutal battle between the Kush and the Assyrian forces that involved tens of thousands of warriors.

On the field of battle, Taharqa ordered his generals to fight in a formation that resembled the shape of a Kushite spear.

Between each spear formation were one elephant, chariot and cavalry brigade. As the Assyrian forces were still forming on the field, Taharqa ordered the Kush to attack.

The Kushite long spear formations containing 30 to 40 men, each armed with sword and spear prepared to advance on the Assyrian line. Each group of spearmen was led by a single warrior whose job it was to breach the enemy's line. Taharqa believed that spreading his men on the field would reduce casualties from the Assyrian bowman in a frontal attack. In a single wave, all the forces of the Kushites and the Assyrians collided in a frenzy of slaughter.

The Kushite bowman filled the sky with arrows as the Assyrian army withered before the Kush. From the Assyrian enemy's flanks came the Kushite cavalry and elephant units that acted to disperse the Assyrian lines of defense. Once the defensive lines were breached, the Kush charged in full force, and the Assyrians were massacred in their retreat.

Taharqa's Greatest Military Blunder

Taharqa wrote, "If your enemy does not respect you, give him ample reason to fear you or he will grind you into dust." With the Assyrians, Taharqa should have heeded his own words.

One year after the Assyrian defeat, they showed their contempt for Taharqa by once again invading Egypt. Taharqa had ample experience fighting and defeating the Assyrians. However, he failed to assess the nature and tenacity of the opposition. After multiple failed encounters with the Kush, the Assyrians kept trying. The relentless Assyrian attacks were a clear sign that only the complete destruction of this enemy would bring peace to the Kush.

Upon defeating the Assyrian army in Egypt, Taharqa should have marshaled his forces and marched to the Assyrian capital with the intent to destroy it. Had Taharqa used this approach, he may have been able to avoid the eventual loss of the Egyptian delta by the hands of the Assyrians.

The Assyrians Regroup and Attack

Even after a sound defeat at the hands of Taharqa, the Assyrian King Esarhaddon was not finished with the Kush. He re-invaded Egypt just one year later, and this time inflicted terrible damage upon the Kush. It is said the Esarhaddon marched his forces as far south as the city of Memphis.

Esarhaddon destroyed much of the city and captured the wife and child of Taharqa. Fortunately for Taharqa, he was able to continue the fight, which reportedly lasted for months. There was much devastation in lower Egypt, but the Kushites managed to hold the lands south of Memphis.

Taharqa was not just a warrior King. He was also known for building multiple monuments and temples, including the restoration and expansion of the Temple of Amun at Jebel Barkal. It was at the mountain of Jebel Barkal that Tarhaqa declared himself with a large golden poster, to be the King of Kings, ruler of the two cobras, and destroyer of the Bedouin.

In 664 B.C, Taharqa died, and the throne was passed to the Kushite Pharaoh Tantamani (Tanta-mani). The Pharaoh Tanta, like his ancestors, ruled over the land of the two cobras. He put this dream into action by invading the areas of Egypt previously devastated by the Assyrians. He succeeded in his efforts to drive the Assyrians from the Egyptian delta.

However, several years after reuniting the two cobras, lower Egypt was again invaded by the Assyrians. This time, the Kushites were pushed back to the second cataract, where they managed to hold their ground once again.

War Against the Occupier

By 655 B.C., the Egyptians living under Assyrian control in the delta began to rebel. The Assyrians were attacked by the Anu- Egyptians looking to free themselves from the occupiers. The Anu-Egyptians managed to defeat the Assyrians, placing lower Egypt back under Kushite rule. Upon the death of the Kushite Pharaoh Tantamani, his son Psamtik I became pharaoh. Egyptologist claim Psamtik I was the creator of the 26th dynasty. How could this be if Psamtik was the son of the previous Kushite Pharaoh? Psamtik would in fact, be a continuation of the 25th dynasty of Egypt.

Psamtik's leadership is relevant because Psamtik I was the son of the so-called last Kushite Pharaoh Tantamani. Psamtik I is credited with reuniting Egypt and is the father of Psamtik II, who ruled Egypt after the death of his father.

The direct royal line of Kushites continued to control Egypt until the time of the Persian invasion. This leadership sequence shows that the Kushite control of Egypt lasted more than two-hundred years. This also means that the alleged 26th dynasty of Egypt never existed!

The Usurper Pharaoh Tefnaht

It might be that the Usurper Tefnaht II began the 26th dynasty after the death of Psamtik I. If this is true, then Tefnaht's control of the delta region was both limited in scope and short in duration. Tefnaht was the father of Nekau I, who died 664 BC in a Kushite reinvasion of the delta region. The pharaoh who replaced him was Psamtik II, the rightful Kushite ruler of Egypt.

Leadership succession is essential because it shows that Kushite control of Egypt lasted a good deal longer than the modern Egyptologist want to admit. My argument becomes even stronger when you consider the pharaonic succession after Psamtik II.

Upon the death of Psamtik II, Ahmose II, son of Psamtik II, became pharaoh. Ahmose II rule was challenged by Apries, a general who declared himself pharaoh during a civil war with the legitimate Kushite ruler. Apries was eventually forced to flee Egypt. The last Kushite pharaoh of Egypt was Psamtik III, son of Ahmose II circa 525 BC.

Chapter 15: The Persian Invasion of Egypt

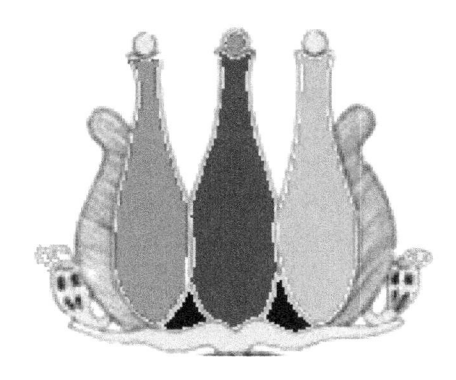

Egyptian Nation in Perpetual Chaos

In 525 BC, the Kushite Pharaoh Psamtik III was defeated by the Persian King Cambyses at the battle of Pelusium. Northern Egypt fell completely under Persian control. The Persians had problems consolidating their rule due to continuing Anu-Egyptian rebellions. After his initial defeat, Psamtik III started a secondary rebellion against the Persians, was defeated, and eventually executed. The Kushite control of Egypt was pushed back to the second cataract of the Nile by the Persian invaders.

Early Persian Control of Egypt

The Persian Cambyses held power for less than two years before more rebellions erupted in Egypt. The Egyptian delta had become a colony for the Persians, and the Egyptians were not happy about this outcome. The Persian leadership did not reside in Egypt. They used their Egyptian territory to extract resources for the greater Persian Empire. The non-Egyptian leaders after Cambyses included Darius I, Xerxes I, Artaxerxes, Xerxes II, and Darius II.

There was a documented revolt lead by a rebel named Amyrtaeus, a person of unclear Egyptian descent. He claimed to be familiarly linked to the pharaohs of the 26th

Dynasty.

Amyrtaeus's rebellion, while successful, was short-lived. Within six years of Amyrtaeus reign, he was challenged, defeated, and executed by the Anu-Egyptian Nefaauid I. Each successive Egyptian pharaoh over the next eighty years were either deposed or assassinated by a subsequent contender. This Egyptian chaos made it possible for the Persians to retake lower Egypt, effectively ending Anu-Egyptian rule.

Kushites Turn Their Backs on Kemet

The Kushites continued to control the lands from the city of Aswan to the Blue Nile. The Persians tried unsuccessfully to uproot the Kush from upper Egypt and finally abandoned the endeavor. By this point, the Kushites had lost all patience with the Egyptians who would use Kushite military resources, then rebel against them and deny their kinship. Worse yet in the eyes of the Kush, the Egyptians had turned their backs on the sacred teachings of the Ma 'at.

The Egyptians accepted the corrupt ways of the foreigners and were no longer a concern of the Anu-Kush. It was the Egyptian loss of their Anu identity that prevented them from ever regaining power in their own land again. This period marked the end of the Anu-Egyptian culture and the beginning of perpetual occupation.

What Happened to the Kushites?

The ruler of Kush at this time was King Amaninatakilebte (Amani-Natakilebte), who reigned from 538 – 519 B.C. He was the son of the Kushite King Anlamaye the Fierce. During this time, the Kush had turned inward to rebuild their nation. This period is known as the Napata period.

During the Napata period, Kushites were building the majority of their temples, monuments, and tombs in the city of Napata, which gave this period its name.

I was only able to find one representation of the Kushite King Amaninatakilebte. See the silver mirror below containing a representation of the King forged into the handle. While this is not the best representation of the King, it is an excellent example of the beauty of Kushite metalwork.

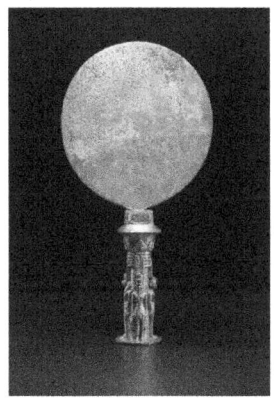

Kushite King Amaninatakilebte Mirror

Kushite King Amaninatakilebte Mirror Handle

Second Persian Challenge of the Kush

There was a period of peace between the Kush and the Persian invaders of Egypt that lasted nearly seventy years. The Kush even contributed archers to the army of King Xerxes II. Under the Persian King Darius III, the relationship between the Persians and the Kush deteriorated. Darius needed resources to build his army to defend against the approaching war machine of the Greeks.

Darius foolishly sought to plunder the Kushites and take their enormous wealth in Gold. Once again, the Kushite northern border that began at Aswan was threatened by a foreign power. The Kushites felt that the Egyptians were too morally weak to be of any benefit, so the Kush prepared to go it alone. The Kushite King Akhraten circa 350 – 334 BC, was furious with the Persians who had begun new incursions into Kushite territory. These actions sparked new friction between the Persians and the Kush.

The following account of the Persian Kushite interaction was written by the Greek explorer Herodotus:

> Herodotus states that the King of Persia wanted to conquer the lands of the Kush and acquire their gold. Darius III sent messengers to King Akhraten of the Kush bearing gifts. The messengers were spies sent to assess the nature and strength of the Kushite King.
>
> King Akhraten realized that the messengers were spies and this greatly offended him. The King berated the messengers and ridiculed the gifts from Darius. In response to Darius, King Akhraten sent the Persian King a Kushite bow with a message.
>
> "When the puny arms of the Persian can draw a Kushite bow with the same ease that I can, then march your forces against the long-lived Kush, and meet your demise."

King Darius was furious at the response of the Kushite King and formed a large army to attack the Kush. The Persians had little knowledge of the Kushite desert and marched unprepared into the no-mans-land during the adverse heat of summer. This territory was very well known to the Kush and was a perilous place for the unprepared.

It had been unusually dry that year, as the Persian army entered the killing zone of the Kushite desert. The Kushite infantry in small bands began sabotaging the food and water sources along the Persian rout.

Kushite archers harassed, trapped, and slowed the Persian advance. When the Persians would send messengers back to their garrisons in Egypt for help, they were intercepted and eliminated by the Kush. As the Persian army entered the most hustle area of the Kushite desert, they ran low on water and supplies.

The Kushite archers began attacking the Persians from all sides, never allowing them to rest or retreat. The army of Darius was trapped for weeks and became so hungry that they began to eat their dead.

On hearing of this carnage, the Kushite King ordered the archers to stand down and allow the Persians to retreat to Egyptian territory. In showing mercy to an undeserving foe, King Akhraten gave meaning to his royal name, which means the "Guardian of Life in the name of God".

Persian Control Ends with Alexander

King Darius returned to Persia when to his surprise, he received an envoy from the Kushite King. The messenger stated that King Akhraten has great respect for King Darius and would like to propose a truce. King Akhraten's proposal was accompanied by gifts of gold, ivory, and textiles from the King who had just humiliated the Persian army.

The Kushite proposal intrigue King Darius who replied that he would talk. During the battles with the Persians, King Akhraten noted an animal brought by the Persians called the Camel. This creature was not known to the Kush at this time. The Kushites noted that the Camel could roam about the desert without water in ways a horse could not. King Akhraten offered to trade goods and gold for more of these remarkable animals.

King Darius had made his own observations of the Kush. The Persian King was impressed at how the Ta-Sety (bowmen) had destroyed his army from a distance. He asked King Akhraten if he might incorporate Kushite archers into his Persian forces. In reality, King Darius was most concerned about the approaching Greeks, but it was already too late.

A bond of trust was reestablished between the Persian and the Kush, and a truce was declared. I speculate that this level of cooperation between two very different tribes is a testament to both the Ma 'at and the Babylonian code of Hammurabi adopted by the Persians. These two codes would have been very compatible, enabling the two great cultures to cooperate.

Within a year of the Kushite Persian encounter, Darius was soundly defeated by the Greek Alexander of Macedonia. After defeating Darius, Alexander's army quickly turned its aggressive intent to lower Egypt, an area controlled by what remained of the Persian forces.

Chapter 16: The Kushite and the Greek

Greeks Replace the Persians in Egypt

Alexander III was a Macedonian Greek who was the son of Phillip II. Alexander acquired the throne of Greece after the assassination of his father in 336 B.C. His primary mission as King was to conquer Persia as revenge for previous military aggression against the Greeks.

Alexander set off with his force of Greek warriors to conquer Persia. After months of combat, Alexander defeated Darius III and became the King of Persia. King Alexander spent the remainder of his reign roaming around Asia and Northeast Africa looking for someone to conquer. Alexander eventually captured a significant portion of the old Persian empire, including lower Egypt. He was declared Pharaoh of Egypt and died shortly after under mysterious circumstances.

It is believed that Alexander died in 323 B.C. in the city of Babylon. He asked to be buried in Aswan, demonstrating the enormous respect he held for Kushite culture.

However, it is believed that Alexander was buried in Babylon where he died. The crown of Egypt was pasted to Alexander's incompetent half-brother, and then to his son Alexander IV. Ptolemy later replaced these two incompetent rulers of lower Egypt.

Ptolemy I Takes the Throne of Egypt

Ptolemy was one of Alexander's most successful military generals and a close friend to the King. After Alexander's death, Ptolemy appears to have disappeared for several years. In 305 B.C., Ptolemy lays claim to the throne of Egypt upon the death of Alexander IV. I hesitate to refer to these Greek leaders as Pharaohs because they were neither Egyptian nor Kush.

It may have been the extensive desert area between the 2nd and 3rd cataracts of the Nile or just good sense that kept hostilities to a minimum between the early Greek occupiers of Egypt and the Kushites. It appears that for several generations, the Greek rulers cooperated with the Kush both economically and religiously. Pharaonic records indicate that the two nations collaborated on trade and temple projects without friction.

Kushite View of the Greeks

By 304 BC, the Kush no longer protected the Egyptians. The nations of the two cobras had finally gone their separate ways. However, the Kush remained a powerful military force that could threaten the Greek's hold on the Egyptian throne.

The Egyptian people did not like the idea of having foreigners claiming themselves Pharaoh or dominating their land. However, they were too weak to mount a frontal attack, although very capable of causing social disruption if not appeased.

Ptolemy's competent leadership temporarily solved the potential Kushite challenge to Greece. Instead of war with the Kush, Ptolemy chose cooperation. The Greek leader also improved the lives of ordinary Egyptians and was respectful of their traditions. This liberal approach to leadership ingratiated Ptolemy to both the Egyptians and the Kush.

Cooperation between the Greeks and Kush was encouraged by the tradition of inter-tribal marriage and temple building. The Ptolemies wisely chose to embrace the Kush rather than attempting to dominate them. Of all previous invaders of Egypt, the Greeks held the greatest understanding and appreciation of the historical role of the Kushite in the creation of Egypt.

Despite the Greek's positives social standing, the Kushites still considered them to be primitive, violent, and materialistic. But to their credit, the Greeks were not socially chaotic like so many of the other Egyptian invaders. The Kushites greatly appreciated the difference!

The Kushites also realized and accepted the realization that Greek leadership was not a follower of the Ma'at. This lack of morality was manifested by relentless power struggles that resulted in multiple murders within the Greek-Egyptian royal family. Even the wives of Greek leadership did not do well among the Greeks of Egypt. In nearly every generation of Greek-Egyptian leadership, assassinations were commonplace.

Tension Began with Ptolemy IV

After more than one hundred years of peace between the Kush and the Greeks, the arrogant Ptolemy IV took the throne of lower Egypt. Tensions with the Kush began almost immediately during his reign. Ptolemy IV accused the Kush of supporting several small rebellions against the Greeks. These revolts were homegrown, ignited by the

Egyptians desire to end foreign rule. These rebellions angered Ptolemy IV, who began hostile acts against the Kush.

Ptolemy IV attempted to dominate the Kush but were utterly unsuccessful. The Kush joined forces with the rebel Egyptian leaders Hugronaphor and later Ankhmakis in the south. They provided food, weapons, and logistics but did not provide human resources to the Egyptian cause. As a warning to the Greeks, each time they attacked the Kush, more of their southern territory would be seized by the Kushites. Ptolemy IV was assassinated in 207 BC, and his son Ptolemy V took the throne of Egypt.

The Return of Female Rule in Egypt

Ptolemy V recognized that fighting the Kush was a losing proposition and wisely encouraged peace between the two kingdoms. Some believe that the true wisdom of Ptolemy V came directly from his wife Cleopatra I, who acted as his co-regent. The Kushites took ample notice of the new female Egyptian ruler who would usher in a long line of Greek female leadership in Egypt.

Upon the death of Ptolemy V, his wife, Cleopatra I, became co-regent for her son Ptolemy VI. There were power struggles within and between the siblings of the Ptolemy's, resulting in a confusing array of leadership. For reasons unknown, each of the successive male Ptolemy rulers appears to have had a female co-gent.

Upon the death of Ptolemy VI, his wife Cleopatra II, daughter of Cleopatra I, took the throne after a revolt she led against her new husband, Ptolemy VIII. Cleopatra II became the sole ruler of Egypt after removing her husband and controlled the throne for fifteen years. Ptolemy VIII was made pharaoh after the death of Cleopatra II.

Cleopatra III, the second wife of Ptolemy VIII, then took the throne before being murdered. For the next fifty years, the Ptolemy line experienced a series of ruthless power grabs at the hands of family members. Cleopatra V and Cleopatra VI, mother and grandmother of Berenice IV, who murdered her husband and took the throne. Berenice IV's death ushered in the famous Cleopatra VII of Caesar, Mark Anthony fame. Cleopatra VII ceremoniously dispatched her brother-husband Ptolemy XIII, her little brother Ptolemy XV, and her sister Arsinoe IV.

A Two-Pronged Family

Egyptologist has speculated that there were two lines within the Ptolemy family. One line belonging to Cleopatra and the other more Kushite line belonging to Arsinoe IV and her brother Ptolemy XV. Arsinoe and her brother opposed Cleopatra VII and her international antics with the Romans. Arsinoe and her brother attempted to remove Cleopatra VII from power which resulted in their untimely deaths by assassinations.

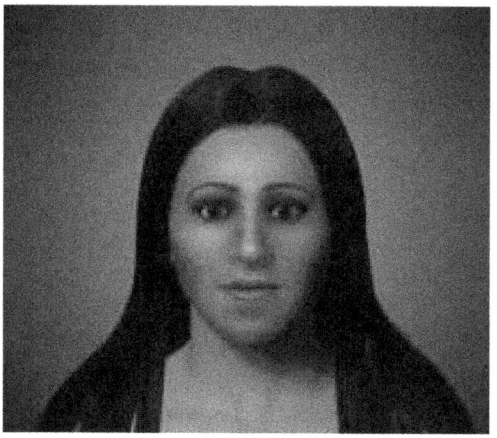

Facial Skeletal Reconstruction of Princess Arsinoe IV

To date, the scientist has been unable to locate the body of Cleopatra VII. Very recently, genetic archeologist believes they have discovered the body of princess Arsinoe buried in a lighthouse shaped tomb in Turkey. The scientist performed a facial reconstruction on the remains of Arsinoe. If Arsinoe's skeletal reproduction is correct, she definitely had both Greek and Anu-Egyptian or Anu-Kushite ancestry.

Kushites Royals Lay Low

During the years of female Ptolemy rule, the Kushite royal family kept a safe distance from the Greeks for fear of being murdered. The reign of the Greeks in Egypt lasted for 300 tumultuous years, ending with the death of the murderous Greek Queen Cleopatra VII.

Cleopatra gave birth to a son Ptolemy XVI, also known as Cesarean. Ptolemy XV was too young to rule the nation of Egypt after his mother's death. Ptolemy XVI disappeared when the Romans enter Egypt in 30 BC.

Cleopatra likeness created from her bust

What Became of the Kushites?

The Kushite Meroitic Phase 3 period began at the time of the Roman invasion of Egypt in approximately 30 BC. The Kushite seat of government and royal palaces are now primarily located in the imperial city of Meroe. Kushite royalty has chosen the city of Meroe in South Sudan as the new capital of the Kushite empire. Meroe is also the Kushite royal's new primary place for burials.

The Kush and the city of Meroe flourish during this period with numerous building projects and the creation of the Meroitic script.

The Kush moved their capital from the northern city of Napata to isolate themselves from the chaos of Egypt. The Kushites were now facing a new and even more corrupt neighbor known as the Roman. The Kushite King, during the Egyptian transition to Roman rule, was believed to have been Arkamani-qo, whose burial pyramid is located in the old city of Meroe.

Chapter 17: The Kushite Verses the Roman

The Roman Parasites of the Nile

After Cleopatra's death in 30 B.C., Egypt was annexed by the Roman emperor Octavian (Augustus Caesar). What little remained of the Kemet nation was once again in the hands of a foreign invader. Under Augustus's leadership, the Romans raped Egypt of its remaining cultural wealth and natural resources.

The Romans used Egypt's agricultural production to feed their armies and the people of Rome, leaving little for the native Egyptians. Augustus quickly began to stamp a Roman identity on the Egyptian culture, which destroyed their indigenous religion and all hope for an Egyptian resurgence.

The Kushites had a harshly negative opinion of the Romans based on their leadership's amoral and violent activities. The Kushite saw in Roman administration arrogance and insatiable greed that would soon focus its power-lust on the Kush.

It wasn't long after Egypt's annexing that the Roman parasites (Nile Leech), as the Kush described them, began coveting the riches of the Kushites. Roman greed and their sociopathic need to dominate others was the catalyst that would ignite the Kushite Roman war.

A Respectful Start

Historical evidence shows that the Kushites and the Romans made an early formal agreement stating that Aswan would be the official northern border of the Kushite Kingdom. The Romans would not attempt to expand their territorial ambitions beyond Aswan or risk war with the Kush. In return, the Kush would not attack the Romans in Egypt or interfere with their corrupt enterprise.

Within five years of Roman rule, the nation of Egypt was in economic turmoil. To understand what was occurring, you need to understand the Roman system of occupation and colonialization.

How the Romans Exploited the World

The Romans are the origin of modern colonialization and nationalistic racism. While the Romans were not the first to invade a nation and attempt to exploit its resources, none were more adept at this approach than the Roman. The Romans convinced themselves that they were culturally and racially superior to others and used their military prowess to enforce their delusion. Modern nationalistic aggression and ethnic slavery can trace its origin to the Roman empire.

The Romans perfected their war machine and colonial occupation at the expense of the Anglos (English), the Gauls (French), Germania (German and related tribes), Barbarians, Carthaginians, Egyptians, Semitics, and Turks. However, the Romans war machine was stopped in its tracks by a female Kushite.

While the Romans called themselves a republic, an empire, and other grandiose terms, in reality, they were little more than an international extortion and protection racket. The extortion part of the crime is activated when the Roman army descends upon a civilization. The Romans used their military to defeat the local militia and subdue the population by setting up a series of forts. The forts acted as a staging ground to attack and intimidate the local communities.

Rome's European ancestors would adopt this same military extortion racket against countless other peoples. Examples of this Roman approach to conquest can be seen in the multi-century aggression against native populations of America, Africa, and Asia.

Once established in Egypt and their forts built, the next step for the Roman was to turn local conflicts to their advantage. This phase of the Roman occupation is exercised by turning one tribe or political group against the other while pretending to support both. The Romans intentionally inflamed local rivalries and provided weapons to the weaker side to attack the stronger. Support of factions dampened the resistance to Roman occupation. These techniques allowed foreign dominance to sustain itself for an extended period. The more prolonged the foreign dominance, the more entrenched the invader became.

After the divisive infrastructure of the extortion racket is in place, the Romans would demand the payment of tribute (taxes). The tribute would often require up to half of the goods produced by the native population. In most cases, these payments would leave the native people poverty-stricken and near starvation. The Romans would also enslave much of the native population using brutality as a means of control. The slave labor was then used by the Romans to build an infrastructure that would further solidify their comfort and control. The Romans also required that young men of the occupied territories had to be conscripted to fight for Rome.

Extraction of Natural Resources

The Roman practice of early extraction of natural resources such as gold, assured that anything of value was shipped back to Rome. Removal of food and other commodities was also an essential Roman strategic move. The Romans used these resources to feed their population in Rome, pay the military, and physically deprive their victims of human dignity.

The Roman tribute or tax forced on the victimized population represents the protection side of the racket. The victim is obliged to pay the tax in order to avoid further Roman attacks. This approach worked so effectively that it became the standard approach used by the European colonialist nations long after the fall of Rome. The Romans were the original state-sponsored criminal enterprise, and nearly all its wealth and power were gained at the expense of some other nation or people.

Did Romans Provide any Value?

Western historians have tried their best to convince themselves that the Roman empire had merit. The real question is, did the Romans add any value to the many civilizations they invaded and destroyed? The honest answer is no! To say yes would assume that there was something inherently inferior about the cultures they conquered. To say yes to Roman contribution also implies that the victims of conquest were somehow deserving of the cruel and inhumane treatment they were forced to endure under Roman rule.

In exchange for Roman tyranny, the victims received violence, deprivation, occupation, aqueducts, cement ports, a colosseum, and crippling taxes. Unfortunately for the victims, the aqueducts, harbors, and fees only benefited the occupiers. The Romans lived on the best land in someone else's nation while sending their fruits of other people's labor back to the city of Rome. Does any of this sound familiar?

The Enemy Makes You Stronger

The Kushites felt that an aggressive adversary like the Romans would make them stronger. The more powerful an enemy, the stronger and more cunning a nation must be to resist that enemy. The Kushites watched and quickly learned Roman weapons and combat techniques and devised unique ways to defeat them.

Roman society was a mess, and this fact did not escape the attention of the Kushites. Throughout the Roman empire, the population was experiencing poverty, war, slavery, rebellions, a rigid social and economic hierarchy, massive injustice, and violent unrest. This kind of social upheaval was common in the Roman world and occurred throughout its entire 900-year history.

A Social Comparison to Rome

The Roman empire was the largest of its time and encompassed the entire Mediterranean Sea. During its 900-year history, the Roman was driven by an extremely perverted need to expand. Romans needed the natural resources and slave labor of others to sustain itself, driving every more expanding conflict in the world.

In the land of the Kush, the people lived in harmony via the Ma'at throughout their entire 8000-year history. The Roman used the sword and extortion to grow their empire while the Kushites used the Ma'at and cooperation. Which of these two civilizations would you define as being the most civilized?

The Meroitic Kushites were busy building a dazzling culture based on the social tenets of the Ma'at (the code of human decency). There was no slavery, exploitation of minorities, brutal sexism, extreme classism, rebellions, starvation, or massive injustice within the empire of the Kush. There was, however, unique and beautiful architecture, care of natural resources, and a general sense of cultural belonging, even if you were an immigrant. The one requirement of all Kushites, was the acceptance of the code of human decency, also called the way of the Kush.

The Kushites felt no need to expand into someone else's territory and steal their resources. The Kushite did not suffer from constant power struggles and assassinations among their leadership. The Kush, if allowed, lived in peace with both its neighbors, the environment, and itself. No, the Kushites were not perfect! But when compared to the Roman, it is crystal clear who had the superior culture.

Chapter 18: The Kushite Warrior Queen

Foolish is he who Underestimates the Strength of the Kushite Female

Not long after the Romans began to impose its will on Egypt, rebellions began among the people. The Egyptians felt that the tribute imposed by the Romans was too excessive. With increasing hunger and discontent, violent confrontations were beginning to break out all over lower Egypt. Several Roman Garrisons were constructed to control the local population, but their police actions further inflame tensions. Again, does this approach sound similar?

The Kushites did not take part in these rebellions against Rome until Rome began coveting the Kushite Gold mines at Wadi Allaqi. At that point, the Kushites began supporting the Egyptian revolts, which greatly angered Emperor Augustus. The Roman Emperor sent a large force against the Kush to take control of their lands.

While there were several notable warrior queens in human history, there is one in particular that stands above all others. The regent of Kush at the time of the Roman invasion was the Kandake (Candice) Amanirenas (Amani-renas). She was known among the Kush as the Warrior Queen. If you're searching for an example of the inherent strength and power of the female spirit, you need to look no further than the story of Candice (Kandake) Amanirenas, Queen of the Kush.

It appears that during the reign of Her Majesty, Queen Amanirenas, she shared power with her coregent uncle or brother Akinidad. Their relationship is not historically clear. Under the direct leadership of the Queen, the Kushites launched a campaign against the Roman occupiers of Egypt, then led by the Roman Prefect Aelius Gallis.

Observation of the Enemy

The Queen sent spies into the enclaves of her Roman enemy to observe their character and their methods of war. In the early skirmishes with the Romans, Amanirenas sent a small military contingent to engage a significant roman force. She noted their weapons, armor, fighting techniques, discipline, and the general sophistication of the Roman war machine.

The Queen quickly assessed Roman strengths and weaknesses. She noted how the Romans repelled each attack and the flaws in their formations. She also noted that the Roman's greatest weakness was their arrogance as they often mocked the Kushite warriors who confronted them.

The Kushite forces under the command of Amanirenas in the west and Prince Akinidad in the east, attacked the Roman garrisons at Syene and Philae, destroying both. The Kushites took many Roman prisoners during these battles and cut their ankle tendons or amputated their hands. The intent of these mutilations was to assure that captured Roman soldiers would never attack a Kushite again.

There is no mention of mass executions or attempts to enslave by the Kush. However, the records do speak of substantial amounts of equipment and treasure taken by the Kushites in these battles.

Stone mask of the Queen Amanirenas

In 24 B.C., the Candice Amanirenas fought several field battles with the Romans, pushing their forces back to their main garrison at Aswan. It is speculated that the queen may have lost her left eye in one of these battles, implying that this lady fought the Romans toe-to-toe. It is written that just before engaging the enemy in combat, Amanirenas would warn the people within the towns and garrisons according to Kushite tradition.

> "If you do not wish to die this day,
> greet me on your knees!"

The Romans built a garrison at the sacred city of Aswan in defiance of the Kush. This action infuriated Queen Amanirenas. Her forces swiped into and destroyed the Aswan garrison killing all who defied her. When the Queen conquered the Romans at Aswan, so heated was her anger that she executed or temporarily enslaved anyone who had cooperated with the Roman. The Queen's actions were highly unusual for a Kushite warrior and were believed to be a warning to those who would collaborate with the Roman parasites.

The Queen also ordered the destruction of every statue and inscription having anything to do with a Roman. She ordered the bust of Augustus taken in this battle, to be buried beneath the floor of her temple palace at Meroe. She chose this location so that anyone entering her palace, including Roman diplomates, would trample upon the head of her despised enemy.

The Battle of Thebes

After taking Aswan, the Queen turned her army north to the city of Thebes. Her conquest of the Aswan garrison forged her reputation as the Kushite Warrior Queen. As her army marched towards Thebes, fear of retribution gripped the entire nation. Egyptians claimed that Amanirenas was so fierce that the Nile crocodile would bow its head to avoid her glance.

To the east of the Roman garrison at Thebes, stood the Kushite forces of Prince Akinidad. An enormous Roman force confronted the Prince. A great battle ensued between the Romans and prince Akinidad on the outskirts of Thebes. The Romans suffered great losses and realized that they could not defeat the Kushite forces. The Queen arrived at Thebes and faced a degraded Roman defender. As the Queen was preparing to attack with the combined army of Prince Akinidad, the Romans requested a truce to negotiate the terms for peace.

Petronius, commander of the Roman garrison on seeing the massive strength of the Kush, capitulated to all Kushite demands. The Romans opened the gates of Thebes and stood idle as the treaty was negotiated. The Egyptian rebellions ended, and taxes were significantly reduced on the Egyptian population.

The Kushites had no interest in ruling the ungrateful Egyptians and left them in the hands of the Romans. The Kush returned to their southern Kingdom, having maintained Aswan as their northernmost border. No tribute was ever paid to the Romans by the Kush. The Kushites kept all captured spoils of the war and warned the Roman to keep to the north of the Kushite kingdom.

Much More Than a Legend

Modern Egyptologists have pathetically disputed the exploits of Queen Amanirenas. These cultural bigots could not bring themselves to believe that the Kushites could have defeated the great Roman army, especially under the command of a woman. However, their arguments abruptly ended when Archaeologist excavated the bust of Augustus buried at the old Kushite city of Meroe. The statue of Augustus was found buried beneath the front gate of Queen Amanirenas's palace, just as the legend had claimed.

It was Queen Amanirenas who first referred to the Roman as the Nile leech or "the Parasites." The leech reference represented the Roman tendency to forcefully suck their wealth and sustenance from the bodies of others. Some believe that it was the loss of her eye that cause the Queen's hatred for the Romans. Others speculate that it was the loss of a beloved warrior, perhaps even a family member, that fueled her rage. Regardless of the reason, I would not want to have been a Roman soldier facing this lady in battle.

More Proof of Her Victories

The building depicted below is the ruin of an Apedemak Temple located in the old city of Meroe. As a reminder, Apedemak is the Kushite god of war. The inscriptions on the face of this temple show two figures, Prince Akinidad on the left and the Candice Amanirenas on the right. These inscriptions represent and commemorate their victory over the forces of Rome.

It is difficult to overemphasize the historical importance of having a female regent depicted on an Apedemak temple. This temple inscription showing a woman smiting her Roman enemies was a first even among the Kush.

Ruins of Queen Amanirenas's Apedemak Temple

Below, is an outline of the temple wall shown above, depicting Queen Amanirenas with swords raised over the defeated Romans. This depiction is absolute proof that not only did this queen exist, but that she also defeated the Romans as the legends have claimed.

Temple wall depiction of Candice Queen Amanirenas's victory over Rome

Several historical records indicate that after the Kushite Roman war, peace returned to the land of the Kush. Apparently, Romans and Kushites had extensive post-war contact and maintained a good social and economic relationship. The victory of the Kush over the Romans is also commemorated on the Stella of Hamadab found just south of the old Kushite city of Meroe. This fierce and exceptionally cunning young queen clearly earned her glorious title as the Warrior Queen of the Kush!

Stella of Hamadab

Did the Kushites Dominate the Egyptians

In nearly every western text I have read about the history of the Kushite, there is a claim that they were domination by Kemet. A detailed review of Kushite history makes these domination theories impossible for me to accept. The argument against this domination theory is simple. If Egypt dominated the Kushites, why were the Kush not invaded and subjugated by the same multitude of enemies that conquered and subjugated Egypt?

Egypt was defeated and colonialized by many foreign nations, none of which were able to defeat the Kush. If Egypt was strong enough to dominate the Kushites militarily, why were they not also capable of protecting themselves from foreign invaders? This question is even more profound when you consider that all of the conquerors of Egypt also attempted to conquer the Kush and failed.

While Egyptian propaganda may claim to have dominated the Kush, the history of Kushite wars points to a completely different reality. It appears far more likely that the Kush dominated Egypt. My argument makes far more sense, especially when you consider and accept the Anu-Kushite origin of the Kemet civilization. It appears that the Egyptian over Kushite domination theory is nothing more than a culturally bias opinion with little or no relationship to truth.

The Invisible Wars of the Ta-Sety

The Egyptians, Libyans, Persian, Assyrian, Bedouins, Greeks, and Romans all tried and failed to conquer the Kush. However, over several thousand years, occasionally, Kushite lands between the second and third cataracts of the Nile were occupied by enemy forces. The Kushites may have won the wars, but they did not win every battle.

When Kushite lands were occupied, a common technique was used by the invader to subdue the Kush. The invader would build a garrison. These forts were placed in a strategic location enabling the invader to send patrols to intimidate the Kushite people.

The general idea was to frighten the Kush into cooperating by using violence and threats against individuals, families, and property. In response, the Kushite initiated an invisible war that made them ungovernable. If there were no local Kushite armies to resist the invaders, the Kush would turn to the Ta-Sety to strike hard at the enemy.

The Ta-Sety is known as the Kushite protector in the shadows or the warriors of justice. The Ta-Sety was not a cult, political group, or formal organization. It consisted of ordinary warriors of both genders who were highly skilled in the Kush's four traditional combat skills. These skills were wrestling (hand-to-hand combat), the sword, the horse, and the bow.

The bow was the assault rifle of the ancient world and the traditional weapon of the Kush. The bow enabled the Kush to defeat entrenched enemies by skillfully using it in asymmetric warfare. The Ta-Sety knew that their strikes would lead the enemy to retaliate, which is precisely what the Ta-Sety wanted. You cannot defeat an enemy until you fully recognize that they are your enemy. Each retaliation, no matter how brutal, would lead to the birth and deployment of more Ta-Sety.

Prepare for retaliation before you strike.
With each attack upon the Kush, strike deeper and harder within the sanctuaries of the enemy.
Give them not a single night of comfort or peace.

The Ta-Sety Vigilante

The Ta-Sety is a Kushite personality type with an unrestrained willingness to slaughter the enemies of the Kush. The Ta-Sety hides among ordinary people and is singularly devoted to the protection of the way of the Kush. The Ta-Sety warrior will attack the enemy to protect the Ma'at and to remain Kush.

Modern Americans might call the Ta-Sety a vigilante because they acted without official authority. The Kushites would argue that the lack of a formal organization is the source of the Ta-Sety's strength. There is no one Ta-Sety head to cut off. The Ta-Sety was an invisible power used to attack and sabotage an occupying force. The Kush admired the Ta-Sety warriors because of their willingness to strike deep into the enemy's heart.

What was most admired was the Ta-Sety's ability to use unique strategies and extraordinary skill to attack a target and inflict crippling devastation.

Chapter 19: The Last Kushite Renaissance

The Rise of Rivals

The Roman takeover of Egypt began in 31 BC and would continue for the next 300 years. While various Roman rulers crowned themselves Pharaoh of Egypt, the authentic culture and character of Kemet had long faded into dust. The Kushites and the Romans, while engaging in occasional conflicts, lived in relative peace for the majority of Roman rule in Egypt. During this period, both the Roman and Kushite civilizations were experiencing profound change and slow-motion decline for very different reasons.

Kushite Meroitic Period

The Mid to late Meroitic period of Kushite history witnessed both astounding cultural achievements and slow cultural decline. During this period, which would last until the 6th century AD, saw growth in Kushite architecture and language even as its territory shrink. The Kush created the Meroitic language during this period and wholly divorced itself from the old Egyptian culture.

The Kushite capital city was Meroe in the south of Sudan, with a slow decline in the importance of Napata, El-Kurru, and other northern Kushite cities. The relocation to Meroe was a clear indication that the Kush did not wish to consistently interact with the Romans, or with what was left of the Kemet.

Constant Border Clashes

Even without the Roman conflict, the Meroitic Kushites were under constant attack by various Bedouin and splinter tribes. These small but regular incursions took a toll on the strength of the Kushite nation and slowly reduced the territory under its control. Over the next three hundred years, the Kushite empire would be reduced to a fraction of its former self. Land once part of the Kushite empire became the homeland of many new nations that rose from the former territories of the Kush. These splinter nations would grow in strength and eventually becoming deadly rivals of their Kushite parent.

From One Kush Came Many Tribes

As mentioned earlier in this text, the Kush was a combination of at least seven significant tribes. During the decline of the Kush, this tribal process worked in reverse. As early as 100 BC, a new nation was formed from the red sea region of the old Kushite empire. This new nation was known as Axum. The Axumites were an aggressive tribe that soon found itself in conflict with the Kushite Medjay on its Western edge. The Axumites eventually consumed the Magi and consolidated its strength.

Another new civilization called the Nobitians was rising on the north-western corner of the old Kushite empire. The Nobitians (not to be mistaken for the Nabateans from Giza) were also a hostile splinter tribe of the Kush. The Nobitians were referred to as the Kushite X-Group culture. They differed from the Kush in that they were mixed with nomadic cultures of the western desert. The Nobitians were one of many groups that had splinted from the old Meroitic Kushite.

Recall the land located between the second to sixth cataracts of the Nile. This area has been traditional Kushite land since the beginning of time. In the 3rd century A.D., the Nobitians began challenging the authority of the Kush in the northwestern region. The Nobitians attacked the Kush from the west, eventually defeating and absorbing their western flank.

Location of Kushite splinter tribes

The defeat of the Kush and the Medjay pushed the influence and control of the Kush further south. Meanwhile, another nation called the Abyssinians had formed to the southeast of Kush. The Abyssinians drove Axum's borders further north, and also pushed Kushite control to the west closer to the Nile.

The Kushites Fight Back

By the 3rd century AD, the Kushites found themselves threatened by four major tribal enemies. These enemies were the Nobitians, Axumites, Abyssinians (Ethiopians), and several Bedouin tribes. The Kush regrouped and attempted to reconquer parts of its old kingdom, beginning with the Nobitian. The Kush was able to defeat the Nobitians and reclaim part of the northern portion of their territory. However, the Kushites were unsuccessful at dislodging the Axumites or the Abyssinians.

A New Religious Threat

In the mid-third century AD, a new religion was swiping

across the ancestral lands of the Kush, approaching it from two directions. To the north of Kush, the Romans had accepted a new faith called Christianity. This new religion was adopted by the emperor Constantine and had become the official religion of the Roman state.

Small Egyptian tribes were also beginning to accept Christianity, slowly influencing the Kush of the north. The Abyssinians were spreading Christianity on the eastern territories of the Kush. Due to the increasing religious influence of small tribes and the Abyssinians, the old pharaonic religion of the Kush began to completely crumble, leading to the rise of the Makurian Kushite period.

Chapter 20: Kushites, Christians and Islam

The Rise of the Makurian Kushites

The Kushite Kingdom slowly declined during the late Egyptian Roman period but continued to exist for another five hundred years after the birth of Christ. The Kushite era after 350 A.D. is referred to as the post-Meroitic or Makurian Kushite period. During this cultural phase, the Kushite Kingdom was on a slow but inevitable decline, as was the pharaonic religion. The wealth and confidence of the nation were on a downward projection, and the people were disengaging.

Romans Did Not Bring Christianity to Kush.

There is a western myth that the Romans under Constantine ushered in the Christian era in the land of Kush. This belief is incorrect! The style and character of the Christian faith accepted by the Romans were far more political than spiritual. Western Christians focused on praising God, wealth accumulation, and the ascent of earthly leaders rather than the treatment of their fellow men. This Roman Cristian characteristic is why the faith failed to keep peace in Europe.

The Kushites would not have accepted a religion designed to glorify gods and earthly leaders at the expense of morality. Christianity in the land of the Kush came from an Abyssinian (Ethiopian) source. The Kush voluntarily accepted Christianity because it did not conflict with the teachings of the

Ma 'at. The Abyssinians were the first Anu-African people to adopt this new faith, which was derived directly from the holy land. The Christian style approved by the Kush was more Gnostic when compared to the Romans, with an emphasis on moral behavior and human decency. Gnostic Christianity was much closer to the teachings of the Ma 'at, which is why the Kushites accepted the religion in the first place.

Kushite Acceptance of Christ

The Kushites did not immediately accept the new Christian religion. Christianity among the Kush slowly gained acceptance, a process that took more than one hundred years. However, once accepted by the Kush, Christianity thrived. However, there were still remnants of the old pharaonic faith among the Kush. The concept of the Ma 'at and the old gods were kept alive in popular Kushite cults. The two most popular religious factions among the Kush were the cult of Ma 'at and Isis. However, the complete collapse of the old Kushite/Kemet language among the Kush spelled the inevitable doom of the traditional Kushite-Kemetic faith.

War alone did not Defeat the Kush

While the Kushites slowly abandoned their old faith and had many enemies, it was not war alone that finally caused the Kingdom to collapse. The Kush was surrounded by tribal splinter groups competing for control over the old Kushite territories. The most threatening of these splinter groups were the Aksumites.

Aksum was now powerful enough to attack the Kush from both the north and the east. The Kushites were used to double front wars, so this alone would not have defeated them. There had to be something else that contributed to the final Kushite demise.

In the 5th century A.D., there were reports of abrupt weather changes, food shortages, and a plague in Egypt. If there were a plaque and weather changes in Egypt, there was probably also climate change and disease in the Kingdom of Kush. With the combination of a double front war, disease, famine and climate change, the Kush could stand no more.

Apocalypse and a New Beginning

It would not be unreasonable to refer to the period between 540 to 620 A.D. as the Kushite Apocalypse. During this period, the Kushites succumb to Axumite attacks, disease, and starvation. What was left of the Kingdom entered a dormant state of hibernation. Yes, hibernation, not total disintegration!

The last of the Kushite Kings to be buried in a Pyramid was King Yesbokheamani, interred sometime in the late 3rd century A.D. However, for the next two hundred years, the Kushite monarchs remained. Candice Lakhideamani, who ruled in the late 5th century A.D., was the last remaining member of the royal house of Kush.

For two centuries before the Kushite national collapse, the Kush was experiencing a slow, steady decline. However, like throwing a large stone into a batch of seeds, the eventual Kushite collapse left a chaotic array of scattered kernels slowly germinating in the warmth of the sun. These cultural kernels of the Kush enabled the fundamental society to survive in various forms for the next eight hundred years.

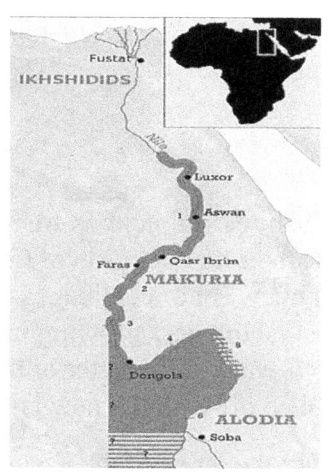

Borders of the Makurian Kushite Kingdom

The borders of the Kush were whittled to a fraction of their former size. An alien faith called Christianity also largely replaced the pharaonic religion of the Kush. The Kushite people were exhausted, frightened, and disillusioned. Despite these dire circumstances, there remained the voices of the Kushite transcenders whispering the moral truth of the Ma 'at. These transcending voices reminded the Kush of who they are, what they were, and what they might become if they remain devoted to the way of the Kush.

The Makurian Kushite and the Arab

By the middle 4th century, the Roman empire had begun to collapse and was no longer a relevant force in Egypt. The Romans had left Egypt, leaving little more than a collection of weak and fragmented tribes. The old temples and monuments of the Kemet were covered in desert sand. From the east, a new national and religious influence called the Arab was emerging. The Arabs quickly conquered Egypt above the first cataract, and the new religion of Islam stormed into the region.

Egypt began to see an enormous influx of Arabs from the eastern Levant. In just a few short years, nearly all of the Egyptian population north of the first cataract had converted to Islam. The introduction of Islam to northern Africa cut off the Kushite Christians from the rest of the Christian world. A conflict between the new Arab invaders and the Kush was inevitable.

The Spread of Islam

The Makurian Kushites still held on to the spirit of the old Ma 'at. However, their new religion of Christianity brought with it an entirely new set of challenges and enemies. Tribes who had accepted Islam were growing in upper Egypt and northern Sudan. It was just a matter of time before the Kushites would face off with the new Islamic invaders.

The Arabs invaded the lands of the Kush in 651 A.D. and quickly pushed into the Dongola region of the Nile. The

Makurian Kushites rallied their troops and forced the Arab army into retreat. Ancient accounts of the battles indicate that the weakened Kushites resorted to the Eye-of-the-fly battle technique to intimidate the approaching Arab army. The Kushite archers rained arrows into the eyes of the enemy from long distances, leaving many dead, wounded, or blind. The Kushites took this form of attack very seriously and even created arrowhead technology solely designed to take out eyes and lodge in the brain of the enemy.

The Kushite eye-of-the-fly technique worked exceptionally well. The Makurian Kush declared that the Arab army retreated like stampeding cattle before them. Routing the Arabs in battle is a remarkable feat given that at this point in history, no other force in the region was capable of defeating the Arab. The combat skills of the Kushite remained legendary despite their enormous decline. So traumatic were these battles to the Arab invaders that they titled the Kushites the (Pupil Smiters) and the (Archers of the eyes).

Makurian Kushite Arabic Treaty

The Makurian Kushites and the Arabs signed a peace treaty called the Baqt in 651 A.D., the same year the war began. The Christian Kushites and the Islamic Arabs swore their covenant upon the Bible, the Koran, and the Ma'at. These three moral texts must have been held in great reverence, as all parties honored the treaty of Baqt for the next seven hundred years. The settlement of Baqt convinced the Kushites that the Islamic Arabs, above all other enemies, possessed integrity and moral consistency.

Islam's Peaceful Conquest of the Kush

By now, you should understand the nature of the Kushite. These people were not about to have any religion or government forced upon them. Over time, Kushites came to admire the Arabs, and many began to convert to Islam. The

Arabs allowed the Christian Kush to be Christian, and the Christian Kush allowed the Arab to be Muslim. The two cultures held each other with great respect, and the two groups lived in harmony in the Nile valley for countless generations. The Kushites and the Arabs possessed a shared morality that encouraged the growth of mutual peace and prosperity.

Religious Hostilities Reemerge

Where humanity is involved, nothing good or bad last forever. It was not until around the year 1360 A.D. that hostilities began to emerge between the remaining Christian Kushites and the Arab Muslim. Keep in mind that there were also Anu-Kushites who converted in significant numbers to Islam.

Despite social turmoil, the Makurian Kushites manage to survive as a nation until around 1400 A.D. Counting the Neolithic period of Kushite history, by 1400 A.D., the Kushites had existed as a contiguous people for more than 8000 years. After 1400 A.D., the northern portion of the old Kushite empire, which included Egypt, had been conquered by the Ottomans. This section of the Ottoman realm was called the Fuja Sultanate of Sennar.

The Fuja Sultanates was also known as the blue sultans. During this period, dark-skinned people were referred to as blue. The Blue Sultanates, with the assistance of the traditional Kushite tribal elders, ruled northern Egypt and parts of Sudan until the mid-1700s. In Sudan, while a minority, the remnants of the various old Kushite Christian tribes remain to this very day.

Chapter 21 - Race and the Ancient Kushite

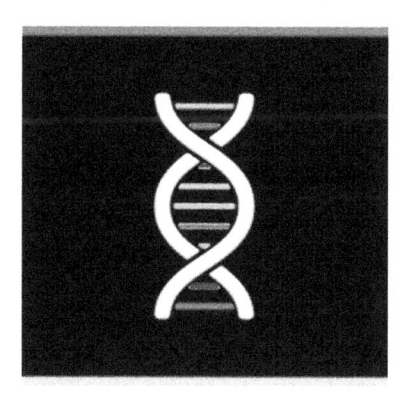

How the Great Kush Navigated Race

In this chapter, we are going to explore the concept of race as the ancient Kemet and Kushites perceived it. I would argue that it is impossible to accurately understand Kushite and Egyptian history using the western perception of race. Western racial beliefs are crippled by a cultural bias that leads to a distorted interpretation of archeological evidence. For example, western racial attitudes have led to a complete disregard for even the possibility of a black African origin of Egypt, a reality I believe to be obvious.

In this text, I have made an extraordinary claim that the Anu (Amelineau), an ancient black African people, were the first to settle the Nile River valley. I've attempted to show that many of the cultural traditions of the Anu were the precursors of ancient Egyptian religion, language, burial practices, and civilization.

I have also argued that if my Anu assumption is true, then black Africans are the creators of both the Kemet and Kushite civilizations. This also means that the Anu created the first known written language and is the true origin of the ten commandments.

A Personal Note Before I Begin

I am a biologist with an extensive background in human genetics and human migratory patterns. In these studies, complex molecules carried in the genetic code are used to trace humanity's movements across the globe. However, I am neither an anthropologist or archeologist, and I humbly concede that my racial origin theory could be wrong. So, to further strengthen my arguments, I will make predictions in this chapter that are related to future genetic and anthropologic findings that will occur in Egypt and Sudan. If my predictions turn out to be correct, then my theories will be considered equally sound, this approach is the nature of science.

The Science of Genetics

Human genetics is a complex study of the human genome. It is a comparison science, which means that the more data you have, the more accurate will be your theories and predictions. The reason genetics is so compelling is that it allows us to extract meaningful stories of our distant past without the need for bias or drama.

The genetic evidence speaks for itself, and the stories it is telling us about humanity are astounding. Some of the most recent genetic data of humankind are so remarkable that I often have trouble believing the evidence before my eyes.

I have discovered to my great amazement that humanity is nothing like we appear to be. While we seem to be exceptionally diverse, we are, in reality, very much the same. The number of things we believe about ourselves that are incorrect is mind-boggling, and the amount of new genetic information about our species is coming in faster than our ability to interpret.

While some of the old scientifically supported beliefs, like man's origin in Africa, are still supported, other theories like that of the family tree are collapsing. We are discovering that humankind is much less linear than we once believed; and that our actual genealogy is far more complex.

What is Race?

Race is generally defined as a group of people who share distinctive physical characteristics. These characteristics are made up of traits such as genetic markers, facial features, hair type, skin color, etc. Race also has a social definition that can encompass vaguely related things like culture, origin, or location. Race can also have multiple interpretations, many of which are arbitrary. The capricious nature of a race is one of the reasons why it's so troublesome as a social or biological concept.

The Concept of Genotype

There is a lesser-known and yet much more accurate biological description of a race. The biological description of race has two components, referred to as genotype and phenotype. A genotype is the genetic constitution of an individual. If a group of individuals is of a similar genotype, they could be said to be a family or a race.

The difference between a family group and a racial group is the size of the population. If the group has ten genotypically similar members, most would call that group a family. If the group has ten million genotypically similar members, you could call it a race. Genotype won't necessarily tell you what a person looks like, but it can tell you what family group derived the person.

A more refined biological definition of race is a group of people who share a common genotype as a result of being part of an isolated breeding or gene pool. As a result of the isolation, these family groups develop common physical characteristics at a higher level than those not within that breeding population. With time, these family characteristics become dominant within the group, and you have the foundation for a race.

Biology finds little value in the category of race because the concept is nondescript and often nonsensical. As this elder has discovered, human perception doesn't always coincide with biological reality. To some of you, all this similarity talk my sound like a bunch of liberal bullshit. But the biological reality shows that humanity has more in common between the races than we do within a race. This genetic omnipotence is especially true within the biologically race known as the black African, who is the origin of all races.

The Biological Concept of Phenotype

What most people think of when contemplating race is the appearance of the person. What a person looks like is referred to as the phenotype. Phenotype is defined as a set of observable characteristics created by a person's associated genotypes and its interaction with the environment. Socially, people are lumped into a hand full of phenotypes and assigned a race. In reality, a race is far more complicated than just one's appearance. A person may appear to be of one race and yet genotypically belong to another. Other problems with a socially assigned race are who gets to pick the traits and how do you interpret the enormous number of overlapping criteria.

Socially Induced Racial Criteria

A problem with using race as a true determent of human differences is the adverse effects of socially induced anomalies. For example, one group believes that it is more intelligent than another. Even if you could element inherent bias, to test this hypothesis, you must still rule out all criteria that can affect the intellectual performance of those tested.

If a group is subjected to poor-quality food or starvation, one would expect less performance. If one group is not intellectually prepared, denied textbooks, subjected to physical hardships, psychologically stressed, or even low expectations, these elements could lower performance. If any of these criteria and a thousand other possibilities are present on the tester, but not the competition, then you cannot make a definitive comparison. In reality, what you would be measuring are the effects of deprivation on a person's intellectual performance, not their actual IQ.

How did Kushites Perceive Race?

How would a people who believed themselves the father and mother of the human race, view race? Certainly not with the same hostility and disconnect observed with parasitic slave cultures like the Romans. This question becomes even more profound when you consider that the Kushites faced the same racial diversity and challenges seen today. The difference is in the brilliant way the Kushites handled race compared to many so-called modern societies.

The Kushite recipe for racial success was human decency and consistent moral vision, heavily seasoned with pragmatism and social justice. The Kushite approach to race is so beautifully practical that you don't even need science to appreciate it!

How Did the Kushite See Themselves?

The following is a firsthand description of how Kushites saw themselves:

"We the Kush, are the fathers and mothers of the human race. The God Amun placed us on this earth first and promised us that we would be on this earth last. We were created in the image and likeness of God, and into this body was placed an immortal soul. We were given enlightenment and the ability to see ourselves. We were given the vision of three-minds (past, present, and future) with the ability to roam the corners of creation. We were given both motherhood and a god phase so that we might exercise the miraculous gift of creativity. We are the essence of humanity and the first among all tribes. We are humankind, we are forever, we are the Kush, the moral human being!"

The Ancient View of Race

Race in the ancient world was not perceived in the same way that race is today. In the time of the Anu-Kush, a race was equivalent to one's tribe. In the Mediterranean, Africa, Mesopotamia, and the Levant, there were many, many tribes. Go back in time 8,000 – 12,000 years to the beginning of the Kush, and the first thing you would notice is human diversity.

While many of these tribes were related, they still had varied physical characteristics. Their differences included hair types, skin color, eye color, nose shape, etc. Wipe from your mind the modern vision that ancient people were homogenous because they were not.

Kushite Historical View of Humanity

The Kushite historical view of humankind starts with their belief that there was once a single tribe that lived in Alkebulan (Africa). The tribes dispersed, migrated and formed many other tribes. Isolated from the mother tribe called the Anu, new tribes formed, some of which looked and acted differently. While this may sound like a primitive view of human history, it's very close to scientific fact. But how do people of the same original tribe come to look and act differently?

The Concept of Family

We think of a family today as one man, one woman, and their children. This primary reproductive group in science is referred to as the core or nuclear family. We can expand on the core family by adding grandparents, aunts, uncles, and cousins, often referred to as the extended family. Now imagine a tribe of extended families made up of perhaps fifteen hundred individuals. Also, imagine that this closely related tribe is isolated from all other tribes.

An isolated tribe will result in a limited breeding population. Those breeding individuals within this tribe have certain family traits. Let's say that this tribe has a range of brown eyes and brown skin color. I use the term range for each named characteristic because the four primary genes (Adenine, Guanine, Cytosine, Thymine) reconfigure themselves, resulting in a variety of characteristics. The result of gene reconfiguration is that no one, not even twins, is exactly alike. No matter who, what or where you are, genetic variation is inevitable.

How a Family Becomes a Race

If the isolated family tribe of fifteen hundred individuals breeds successfully and grows in number, eventually, you will have a sizeable closely related gene pool. We might refer to this group as a large tribe, but you could just as easily call this group a race. Why? This remote tribe only breeds with itself. Scientist refers to this circumstance as an isolated gene pool.

A secluded gene pool results in a large group of tribal members who share family traits, which happens to be the phenotypic definition of race. The definition of race is a group of individuals who share specific physical characteristics or traits as viewed by society. Therefore, a race could be considered a large family that only breeds among its members. The truth is, an isolated gene pool is equivalent to large scale incest. Yuck!

Expanding the Tribe

All tribes fear the unknown, which limits their evolutional growth. Hypothetically, a family of one-hundred-fifty gray skin, green-eyed individuals approaches a much larger brown skin, brown-eyed tribe. Both tribes are the same species that we'll call (human beings).

The brown-eyed tribe will immediately determine that the gray skin green-eyed individuals are not part of their tribe or race. The larger brown-eyed tribe will be left with three options. The brown-eyed tribe can murder the gray-green eyed tribe, isolate and control them, or accept and breed with the gray-green eyed tribe. Each of these choices has advantages and disadvantages.

The first option is to destroy the gray green-eyed tribe. The massacre option is especially popular with the immoral, paranoid, racist, and stupid members of the brown-eyed, brown skin tribe. The reality is, the brown-eyed tribe will probably make their decision based on the level of perceived threat. If the threat is perceived to be low by the brown-eyed tribe, the second option will come into play.

The brown-eyed tribe attempts to isolate and observe the gray-skin green-eyed tribe. Since isolation, observation, or oppression can't last forever and causes conflict, the wise within the brown-eyed tribe will consider the third option. The third option is not only the easiest, but it's also the most enjoyable. Someone within the brown-eyed tribe is going to breed with one or more members of the green-eyed family. You can bank on it! This breeding reality introduces several evolutionary possibilities for both tribes.

Breeding with the gray-skin green-eyed tribe will introduce the gray-skin green-eyed trait into the brown-skin brown-eyed tribe and visa-versa. While both tribes already contain the characteristics of both tribes as a recessive trait, the offspring will be perfectly viable but more diverse. Mixed mating allows recessive traits to more easily manifest themselves within both tribes, resulting in a stronger and more diverse gene pool.

Acceleration of Tribal Evolution

Now here is a theory the racist will not enjoy reading! Humankind, like all other living things upon this earth, is in a state of continuous evolution or change. Rather you believe in evolution is irrelevant and will not affect the reality of genetic recombination and adaptation. The evolutionary process usually takes hundreds, if not thousands of years, and without it, a species will experience an abbreviated existence.

The most potent form of human evolution is tribal interbreeding. Among tribes, several factors limit human interbreeding slowing the evolutionary process. These factors range from personal preference to social isolation. The natural state of tribal evolution was slow in the early history of humanity because of distance isolation. However, modern humans of all tribes are everywhere, which will result in an accelerated evolutionary process.

Tribal Interbreeding. Good, Neutral or Bad?

Tribal or Racial interbreeding is good because it speeds up the human evolutionary process. It's neutral in that you may not see the positive results immediately and bad in that some combinations may have undesirable genetic characteristics. If you believe that speeding up genetic recombination is somehow wrong, then you will resist interbreeding. Most arguments for resistance are based on superficial social factors like appearance, power, or tradition. However, these superficial social concerns have no relevance in biology.

Genetic evolution is concerned with the physical, intellectual, creative, and adaptive characteristics of the human species. Theoretically, these biological factors are enhanced through racial (tribal) interbreeding. This is not to say that some breeding combinations may result in an undesirable outcome. However, it's important to note that an adverse outcome is possible with any reproductive combination.

Why is Tribal Interbreeding Best?

To my knowledge, there has never been a study of all the possible combinations of inter-tribal reproductive offspring. The reason for this is the enormous number of existing combinations. There has already been so much tribal genetic recombination in our species, that it has already resulted in too many tribes to evaluate.

All of us who exist today are the product of multiple episodes of tribal interbreeding that occurred in the recent and distant past. The fact that humanity exists in its current form and mass is definitive proof that tribal (racial) interbreeding works exceptionally well. In the biological sciences, anything that works well will prosper in nature.

The Bogus Concept of Racial Purity

When one speaks of race in today's society, they are usually using appearance as their racial identifier. The problem with this approach is that appearance is only half the story. Appearance also has social connotations having nothing to do with reality. Racial categories are incorrectly used to describe a group of people with similar physical characteristics who may or may not be biologically related. Identifying a race can be extremely tricky. At best, racial categories can be used to treat specific diseases. At worst, racial categories are used to stereotype, discriminate, and attack others.

Most people are not qualified to identify anyone's race. For example, if you consider yourself black and you live in America, can you honestly identify the racial differences between a Chinese and a Japanese? If you identify as white, can you honestly identify a Sudanese person from a South African? How about an East Indian from an Arab? Without the cultural identifiers to assist us in identification, the untrained eye usually does not know what race (tribe) they're viewing.

I confess that minus social clues and stereotypes, I can barely tell one white tribe from another, and I know genetics. If you've got red hair, I might think you're Irish. However, you could just as easily be French, Italian, German, or Syrian. One of the reasons racial identity is flawed is that we are all a combination of many races. There is no such thing as a pour race, but there is such thing as tribal bias (racism). The idea of racial purity is a social construct designed to isolate, exploit, and discriminate against those you consider to be of less social value than yourself or others like you.

How to Create a Race

A race is an extremely fragile concept that can be changed with a single mating. In basic genetics, when you cross two biological objects of the same species, the result of this mix follows a simple pattern called the 25/50/25 Rule. Please note that the 25/50/25 rule is a gross oversimplification used to make this concept easier to understand. Believe it or not, this simple rule works pretty well in mammals, and it enables you to predict the appearance of an offspring without any training in molecular biology.

The 25/50/25 Rule – using skin color as an example, means that 25% of the offspring will exhibit a skin color that is closer to the darker parent. Another 25% will exhibit a skin color closer to the lighter parent. Fifty percent of the offspring will present a skin color <u>range</u> that is a medium of the two parental extremes. The 25/50/25 rule also works for a thousand and one other human traits between a mating pair.

Purity was Never a Good Idea

Genetic studies have shown that a human isn't even pure human, let alone racially pour. We are all made up of at least three other creatures that were similar to us, but not Homosapien. We had sex with these now-extinct creatures, and all of us, to some extent, carry their genes today.

What we think of as human purity is in genetic terms a terrible idea. To assure healthy offspring, you need a large gene pool that contains a significant amount of genetic diversity. As most know, mating with your sister or brother can result in an unpleasant outcome both socially and biologically.

When humanity tries to breed purely, biology rewards us with a dull mind, a clubfoot, or a hunchback. (I in no way wish to imply that these disease states represent bad breeding). However, if any of these three unsightly characteristics are in your immediate family, your offspring could share these genes. Nothing personal, King Tut! Both the Egyptians and the Kushites noticed this trend in their royal families. The Kush believed that nature was trying to warn them of the perils of purity. Sadly, the purity lesson was ignored by some Egyptian dynasties who sadly, experienced disappointing results.

The closer you are to your mate, the more likely the offspring will experience some form of harmful mutation. On a more extensive scale, people can also suffer from group incest, where there is not enough genetic diversity within the population. One of the signs of low tribal diversity is a group-specific disease or progressively lower birth rates. Lack of genetic diversity can result in a hidden vulnerability that results in the slow extinction of an entire population.

Where Kushite-Egyptian Conflicts a Race War?

You would think all conflicts between Egyptians and the Kushites were race wars if you accept the bias views of some Egyptologists. These poorly informed scientists often interpret history as if there is some magical racial line between the Egyptians and the Kush. Humanity doesn't work that way! The truth is, there were no race wars between Egyptians and Kushites because they were fundamentally the same race.

The racial cohesiveness of the two nations was especially evident before the first commercial invasions. People do change depending upon their breeding population. When new mating sources enter a population, it does not take long before people take advantage of this new sexual resource.

In 3150 B.C., there was an Egyptian war of independence led by the Pharaoh Menes, who was ethnically Anu-Kush. The fight was over Egyptian autonomy, a civil war if you will, having nothing to do with race. But what of the Egyptians after the separation from the Kush?

After the separation from the Anu-Kush, the Anu-Egyptian civilization thrived for Millennia. During that time, the Egyptian and Kushite states grew in commercial sophistication. The major cities of both nations became cosmopolitan hubs that attracted other ethnic groups from around the known world. The majority of foreigners settled in the delta and northern areas of Egypt and then migrated south. The presence of new and exotic breeding opportunities is nearly irresistible to the human species.

Early Commercial Migration

Migration for commercial purposes was also happening in the area between the 2nd to 4th cataracts of the Nile. This area placed foreigners in direct contact with the Kushites. Over hundreds of years, people in this region heavily interbred. Like cream slowly trickling into a cup of black coffee, the Egyptians and the Kush gradually changed over time. Not only were the Egyptians and Kushites culturally influenced by foreigners, but they were also changed physically (phenotypically). The Egyptians were altered more than the Kushites during this commercial period because they were of a loose sexual nature. I'm kidding!

Forced Interbreeding through Conflict

While interbreeding of tribes occurred in both the Egyptian and the Kush, the Kush were never coerced. However, the first invasion of Egypt significantly increased involuntary inbreeding within their population. Unlike the Kush, the Egyptians were defeated by many outside invaders. Over time, these invaders interbred with Egyptians in far greater numbers. These same invaders never conquered the Kushites, so the Kush were not subjected to forced intermingling.

In any event, racial intermingling with other tribes while it certainly occurred, was not required to change the Kush. The Kush already possessed several natural altering forces like inherent genetic diversity, genetic mutation, secondary migration, and adventure. Each of these elements provided a source of natural diversity seen among the Kushites. Despite the above evolutionary aspects, the Kushites remained fundamentally Anu (black African-Asiantic) for the majority of their long and distinguished history.

All of Humanity Exist Within the African

The original Kushites were phenotypically (social, physical appearance) black African. More accurately, the Anu-Kushite was a mixture of several different kinds of black African tribal groups. The word black is defined here as all people of African ancestry with pigmented skin.

The Kushites had many different skin colors from red-black to very light brown. The reality of the human species is that skin pigmentation is a palette of colors that cannot be accurately described with terms as simplistic as black or white. The terms black, white, brown, etc., are social definitions that are loosely associated with one's skin color and race.

Black African people have the most diverse genome on the planet. It is not unusual for the members of a Kushite family to have multiple shades of brown skin. There is no characteristic in humanity that does not exist in a dominant or recessive form within the African genotype. If you were to evaluate any indigenous African, Afro American, or Afro Brazilian nuclear family today, you'd see the same dynamic skin color variations common among our many genetically related African tribes.

The Many Shades of the Kushite

In the land of the Anu-Kushite/Anu-Egyptian, an ethnic cream was being added to an ethnic coffee. In the Americas today, ethnic coffee is being added to an ethnic cream. The outcome of these mixtures will result in precisely the same physical diversity.

The word diversity is kryptonite to the mind of a racist, but mother's milk to the soul of the Anu-Kushite. The Anu need not fear diversity because it has always been a part of who we are.

Four of the 98 shades of the Kushite

Like those of African ancestry today, the Kushites were a people of great physical diversity even without outside biological influence. The inherent differences within African people provide the genetic material needed to create all human phenotypic characteristics. So natural is diversity within the Anu, that it can be summarized in a simple poem:

> There is but one shade of
> black and but one shade of
> white. But there are 98
> shades of the Great
> Kushite!

The above poem not only refers to one's physical appearance, but it also applies to the quality of one's morality. There is nothing in the appearance of a human being that is remotely indicative of that person's level of or commitment to righteousness. This is why the Kushite defined themselves as the moral human being, not the black or brown human being.

The Kushites were a family of people just like any other tribe. As previously mentioned, before there was a formal Kushite kingdom, there were at least seven other distinct tribes that would one day become the great Kush. All seven of the original tribes of the Kush, plus countless smaller and foreign tribes, all contributed to the physical characteristics of the Anu-Kushite and the Anu-Egyptian.

Interestingly, the Kushites felt that the darker an individual's skin color, the closer that person was to the majesty of the Gods and the purity of the original Anu. However, the true morality of a person could only be judged by their adherence to the Ma'at and the Kushite trilogy of truth. Among the Kush, it was the morality of a person, not their appearance that determined superiority.

Chapter 22: Race of the Egyptian Pharaohs

Phenotypic Clues to the Race of the Pharaohs

Egyptologists often refer to the (age or dynasty) of the black pharaohs to describe a period when the Kushites conquered Egypt. I mentioned earlier that I have a problem with this description because it implies that the other pharaohs were not black. This assumption is willfully incorrect! Since I lack the genetic profiles of the ancient pharaohs, I'm forced to use physical appearance (phenotype) as my guide. While physical appearance is not definitive of a person's race, it can be indicative.

Race of the Royal Families

For millennia, it was a tradition among the royal families of the Egyptians and the Kush to create alliances through marriage. Alliance marriages were considered by the Kush to be a peaceful opportunity to expand their political influence and their gene pool.

Kushites took brides from the royal families of every known region of the ancient world. Alliance marriages were arranged between the Kush and the Hyksos, Libyans,

Bedouins, Persia, Assyria, Greeks, various Semitic groups, and Eurasians. Alliance marriage was an effective way of keeping the peace and promoting trade. You would expect that some of these alliance marriages would produce royal children of mixed heritage.

This political form of genetic expansion is strongly represented in the stone likenesses of many ancient pharaohs. Stone busts also argue against the belief that there was a distinct racial difference between the ancient Egyptians and the Kushites.

Anu Origin of the Kemet

I have consistently argued that the Anu (black African) was the origin of Egypt. The early Egyptians were phenotypically black, just like the Kush. The Anu-Egyptians were Kush, and the Kush was Anu-Egyptian. This undeniable fact has been sitting under our noses for centuries. So how is it that so many of us have a European image of the Egyptians?

Two European tribes conquered Egypt and declared themselves pharaoh. One of the most successful of the European tribes to capture Egypt was the Greeks. The Greeks ruled Egypt for three hundred years adopting and contributing to Egyptian culture. But the Greeks were not Egyptian by custom or by race. I would argue that the day the Greeks took control of Egypt was the same day Egypt ceased to exist.

During the reign of the Greeks, Egyptians mounted multiple rebellions to remove them from power. Although these rebellions failed, they remain as proof of the Egyptian desire to free themselves from foreign rule. The Greeks were a foreign invader of Egypt and had no familial relationship with it. The only conquers of Egypt that had a familial relationship with Egypt was the Kushite.

Romans were Even Less Egyptian

The Roman invaders of Egypt were also not Egyptian by culture or by race. The Romans dominated what was left of Egypt after the Greek collapse. The Romans ruthlessly exploited the people of Egypt without benefit to the Egyptians. It is through the Roman eye that we depict Egypt today, which provides a distorted view of the true nature and origin of Egypt.

The Racial History of Egypt

In the deep expanse of time long past, various Anu tribes arose in the area of the Sahara-desert. The Anu precursors of Egypt migrated from the Sahara and settled in the land from the Nile Delta to the Dongola Reach in Sudan. The Anu also migrated to the west and south of the Sahara. These other directional migrations would later form into various black African tribes.

Representation of the Ancient Anu

The Amelineau (Anu) created the cultural foundation of both the Kemet and the Kush. The Anu made their homes along the northern and southern Nile River valley. The ancient Anu may have entered the Nile valley before 8000 B.C. forming the bases of what would become the ancient Kushite and Kemet cultures. No one knows why the Anu migrated from the Sahara or the south. The Anu migration may have been the result of climate change causing the desertification of the Sahara. The migrations may just have easily been the result of war.

Racially, the Anu were black Africans of dark red-brown to light brown complexion. I would not doubt that the Anu were themselves a mixture of various African family groups. Phenotypic diversity had already begun in the Sahara region thousands of years earlier. You could call the Anu the origin or first phase of Egyptian/Kushite evolution.

Second Phase of Anu Racial Evolution

The Anu gradually created the cultural precursors that would later become the Kemet and Kushite nations. The Anu was highly successful and created a prosperous society. The prosperity of the Anu attracted other tribes from the Levant, which promoted racial and cultural exchange. It could be that a peaceful commercial process drove the first racial evolution of the Anu.

Third Phase – Birth of the Anu-Kemet

The process of genetic recombination escalated after the Anu-Kemet war of independence from the Anu-Kush. Recall the face of the first pharaoh Menes and his war of independence.

Menes, the first Pharaoh of Egypt

After the Anu-Egyptian war of independence in 3150 B.C., the Anu-Egyptians politically separated from the Anu-Kush. Immigration from outside tribes continued to enter and mate with both Anu-Egyptians and the Anu-Kush for millennia. Over the next fifteen hundred years, both the Anu-Egyptian and the Anu-Kush would phenotypically evolve while remaining Anu.

To further strengthen my argument that the Anu (black Africans) are the origin of Egypt, I've decided to show you the Anu-Egyptian heritage of the early Pharaohs. I will begin with Menes, the first Pharaoh of Egypt. I have provided several sculptural representations of the most important pharaohs of ancient Egypt to show that most our phenotypically Anu.

The Pharaoh Djoser 2670 BC

The Pharaoh Djoser is an Anu-Egyptian pharaoh who has been credited with building one or more of the early step pyramids of Egypt. What is clear is that Djoser, like his predecessors, was phenotypically Anu.

Below is another sculptural representation of an early Anu-Egyptian Pharaoh named Huni. He is also credited with building one or more of the early cultic pyramids. What is clear is that Huni, like Djoser, was phenotypically Anu.

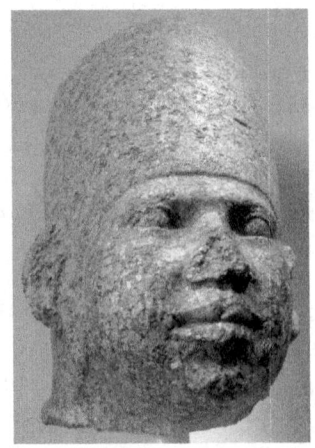

The Pharaoh Huni 2637 – 2613 BC

You might be wondering what's with the chipped noses on the pharaoh statues. These acts of vandalism were deliberately done for two reasons. The first was to interfere with the pharaoh's recognition in the afterlife. The other reason was an attempt to mask the Anu (black African) heritage of the ancient Egyptian leadership.

Pharaoh Khufu, builder of the Great Pyramid 2589 BC

Khufu is believed to be the most likely builder of the great pyramid, and he too is phenotypically Anu. What this means is that it was the Anu (Black African) who originated the pyramid building culture on the African continent. As previously mentioned, after the Anu-Egyptian Anu-Kushite political separation of 3150 BC, there was no separation of the populations. What changed was the Anu-Egyptian formed a separate line of Kings, which amounts to a political separation, not ethnic.

The Anu-Egyptians also no longer had the combined strength of the Kush for protection against the outside world. The Anu-Egyptians responded to this challenge by building a formidable military force that kept them safe for sixteen hundred years. The Kushites, who controlled upper Egypt from Aswan to the Blue Nile, did the same.

Fourth Phase of Anu-Egyptian Racial Evolution

During the post-independent period of the Anu-Egyptian, they continued to experience peaceful commercial immigration from many lands, as did the Anu-Kush. However, the Anu-Egyptian experienced far more migration from the Levant due to its proximity to the north. This closer proximity added a higher concentration of Afro-Asiatic (Sematic) tribes to the Anu-Egyptian population.

What happened next is not surprising. The Anu-Egyptian and several Semitic groups interbred, resulting in more phenotypic variation.

Djedefre, son of Khufu 2566-2558 BC

The Anu-Kushites to the south of Egypt experienced less interbreeding with sematic tribes compared to the Anu-Egyptians. The Anu-Kush experienced more interbreeding with black African tribes to the south and west of the Nile. This difference in breeding population resulted in a temporary phenotypic stabilization among the Anu-Kushites.

More Examples of Anu-Egyptian Pharaohs

Before moving to the next phase of racial evolution within Egypt, I'd like to provide a few additional examples of what are obviously Pharaohs who are phenotypical black African.

Khafre built the second largest pyramid at Giza

The Pharaoh Menkaure 2532 BC

The Pharaoh Menkaure is responsible for building the third largest pyramid at Giza. We have now established that the three largest pyramids on the Giza plateau were built by Anu-Egyptians.

The Pharaoh Pepi I 2332-2282 BC

Mentuhotep II 2060 – 2010 BC

Mentuhotep is the pharaoh who begun the eleventh dynasty.

The Pharaoh Senusret I 1971 – 1926 BC

The Pharaoh Senusret I in the picture above proudly sporting his Kushite Afro hairstyle. This long-lived pharaoh was followed by his son Senusret II shown below.

Senusret II 1897 - 1878 BC

The New Ma'at

Amenemhat III 1860 – 1815 BC

Sobekhotep VI - 1725 BC

Please note that each of the Anu-Egyptian Pharaohs depicted above was a first, second, third, and even sixth generation. These generational links imply that Anu-Egyptian leadership was common before the coming of the Hyksos invasion.

Fifth Phase – Forced Egyptian Racial Evolution

The fifth phase of Anu-Egyptian integration was implemented by force. This new influx of genetic material came to Egypt during the invasion of the Hyksos. The Hyksos are believed to have originated from an area that ranged from the costal Levant to what would be today's nation of Turkey. The Hyksos invaded the northern Egyptian Delta region around 1650 B.C.

For the next 100 years, the Hyksos, Egyptians, Kushites, Canaanites, Jews, and other people of the Levant were practicing intense genetic recombination. There was also new genetic input coming to Egypt from central Africa and the desert Bedouin tribes. The result of these sexual encounters was an increasing amount of racial diversity (gene recombination) and phenotypic change among the Anu-Egyptians and the Anu-Kushites.

The Hyksos never defeat the Kushites or successfully invade their lands. The Anu-Kushites were a formidable military force that could not be defeated by the Hyksos. The Kushite's military prowess resulted in less interbreeding with the Hyksos when compared to that of the Anu-Egyptians.

Sixth Phase - Resistance to the Hyksos

After approximately 100 years of Hyksos domination, the Egyptians began the Theban revolt in the year 1551 B.C. However, by this time, the Hyksos was well integrated into the Egyptian breeding population. With the assistance of the Kushites, the Hyksos were defeated, and Ahmose I founder of the 18th dynasty became pharaoh. The Ahmose's revolt restored Anu-Egyptians to the throne of Egypt, who by this time were mixed with considerable Hyksos ancestry.

The Pharaoh Amenhotep I

I do not have a good likeness of Ahmose I, but the above picture is a statue of his son, Amenhotep I. This pharaoh appears to be of mixed heritage, which is not at all surprising given the history described above.

Rebel Anu-Egyptian Queen expelled by Hyksos and protected by the Kush.

After the defeat of the Hyksos, Thutmose I expanded Egyptian territory into the Levant. Thutmose II attempted to expand Egyptian territory into the land of the Kush. Upon failing, and with the wisdom of Hatshepsut, a peaceful relationship was formed with the Anu-Kush. This respectful approach to relations with the Kush gave Egypt commercial access to the Anu-Punt and lands further south.

The new Egyptian Kushite alliance was sealed by marriage, reinjecting Anu-Kushite heritage into the royal line of Egypt. This relationship can be seen in the faces of the pharaoh Amenhotep II, and his son Thutmose III.

The Pharaoh Amenhotep II

Seventh Phase - Restoration of Anu-Egyptian Rule

By the reign of Thutmose IV, Anu-Egyptians were once again in firm control of the Egyptian nation. Their closer relationship with the Kushites leads to Amenhotep III, son of Thutmose IV.

Amenhotep III was of Kushite descent and followed the teachings of the Ma 'at. He came to be known as the Magnificent Pharaoh.

Amenhotep III – The Magnificent Pharaoh 1390 - 1352

Why do I believe that Amenhotep III was a mixed race Kemet Kushite using proof other than his facial features? Please note Amenhotep III's crown. Notice that the crown contains the double Uraeus, which implies his Kingship over both the Egyptians and the Kush. This finding means that Amenhotep III was able to unify the lands of the two cobras peacefully. It's no wonder he was known as the magnificent pharaoh!

Subsequent Pharaohs like Amenhotep III's son Akhenaten brought chaos to Egypt and the Kush by challenging the old religion in favor of a single god Aten (Aton), the sun god. This action caused a rift between the Egyptians and the Kush, which resulted in another separation.

By the time of Tutankhamun, son of Akhenaten, the Egyptian pharaohs no longer ruled over the Kush. Akhenaten's religious transition ended his control of Kush. How do I know this? Please notice the crown of Tutankhamun (next page). The crown <u>does not</u> contain the double Uraeus, which has been replaced with the symbol for the god Horus.

Tutankhamun 1335 – 1332 BC

Tutankhamun was a young, weak pharaoh who was usurped by Ay, his chief advisor. It is not clear if Tutankhamun was murdered. He was in such poor health that he might have died as a result of an injury.

After the short reign of Ay, the none-royal general Horemheb became Pharaoh. Horemheb is best known for destroying temples and monuments associated with the Pharaoh Akhenaten's Amarna period. Horemheb was followed by the Pharaoh Ramesses I.

The most famous Pharaoh in the long line of pharaohs named Ramesses was Ramses II. Ramses II is known as the Pharaoh, who fought the Hittites to a draw.

While Ramses II claimed to have dominated the Kush, I don't believe this assertion for one second. Ramses II was known to exaggerate his accomplishments using propaganda. Ramses II was also dethroned during his reign. However, the most persuasive evidence of Ramses II's lack of dominance over the Kush is his crown, which does not contain the double Uraeus.

Ramses II 1279 – 1213.

Ramses II recovered power and lead Egypt for nearly fifty years. His long reign enabled him to become one of Egypt's most prolific builders. For the next seven hundred years, Egypt's fortunes ebbed and flowed.

For several centuries after Ramses II, the nation of Kemet was being peacefully undermined by the Libyans, who eventually took control around 943 BC. After years of chaos, the Libyans were becoming a nuisance to the Kushites.

Eighth Phase – Anu-Kushites Conquer Egypt

In 720 BC, the Kushites were led by an enigmatic ruler named Piankhi, son of King Kushta, the Great. In 714 B.C., the Egyptians were invaded and conquered by Piankhi, one of the greatest of the Kushite Kings. The Pharaoh Piankhi was the second pharaoh of the two cobras, with the first being the magnificent Pharaoh Amenhotep III. Piankhi reintroduced Anu-Kushite control of Egypt, which remained stable until the time of Ahmose II 570 BC.

The Kushite Pharaoh Piankhi, Lord of the Two Cobras

Two-hundred years later, the Anu-Kushite, who ruled Egypt, was invaded by the Assyrians. The Assyrians pushed the Kush back to the first cataract of the Nile. The Assyrians added another genetic layer to the Egyptian population, although they did not last long. Within twelve years of Assyrians victory, they were removed from rule. The Anu-Egyptians rebelled the Assyrians but were unable to entirely remove them from Egypt.

The Anu-Egyptian pharaoh Ahmose II, also known as Amasis II, ruled for nearly forty-five years. He was the last of the great Kushite-Egyptian pharaohs to reign before the Persian invasion of Egypt.

The son of Ahmose II, Psamtik III came to power in 526 B.C. Psamtik III rule for less than one year before being defeated and executed during the first Persian invasion. The Persians also removed the remaining remnants of the Assyrians and took complete control of the Egyptian territories to the second cataract. The Persians attempted to conquer the Kush and failed. After a period of about three years, the Egyptians rebelled against the Persians. With the help of the Kush, the Persians were temporarily expelled from Egypt.

The Kushite Pharaoh Ahmose II, 570 – 526 BC

Ninth Phase of Anu-Egyptian Racial Evolution

The Persians reinvaded Egypt and took control from 484 – 332 BC. During the period of Persian rule, Egypt experienced multiple rebellions and purges of leadership. Occasionally during this same period, native Egyptian rulers managed to take back the throne. However, these pharaohs were relatively weak and under the ultimate control of the Persian Kings. Many Persians migrated to Egypt, and a new source of gene recombination began. There is also evidence that Persians and Kushites also interbreed. These Kushite-Persian relationships were formed primarily as a means of keeping the peace between the two nations.

Tenth Phase of Anu-Egyptian Racial Evolution

In 331 BC, The Greeks defeated the Persian empire and entered Egypt under the command of Alexander III. Within a year, Alexander died in Babylon under suspicious circumstances. It is rumored that Alexander requested that he be buried in Aswan, the sacred city of the Kush.

The Ptolemy dynasty began in Egypt within a decade after Alexander's death, and they ruled for the next three hundred years. The Greeks adopted Egyptian culture and interbred with the Egyptian royal family and, to a lesser extent, the general population. The Greeks also had extensive contact with the Kush. In the early phase of the Greek takeover of Egypt, peace with the Kush was the norm.

More than a century later, under Ptolemy IV, the Greeks attempted to attack the Kush. Greek aggression against the Kush quickly failed, and peaceful relations were restored. The Greeks were highly cooperative with the Kushites, often joining them in the building of temples and monuments. Despite their cooperation, the Greeks were neither Egyptian nor Kush.

Eleventh Phase of Anu-Egyptian Racial Evolution

The next phase of Egyptian racial evolution came in the form of the Roman invasion. The Romans did not need to fight their way into Egypt. The Roman leader Octavian defeated his rival Mark Anthony who had allied with the Greek-Egyptian Queen Cleopatra VII. Upon the defeat of Mark Anthony, Cleopatra committed suicide.

Cleopatra had already murdered her sister and brother leaving only her infant son as the possible heir to the Egyptian throne. This circumstance enabled Octavian, retitled Emperor Augustus Caesar, to remove his young rival and annex Egypt after Cleopatra's death in 30 BC.

The Kushites in 30 BC were in their Meroitic renaissance period and were neither impressed nor intimidated by the Romans. The reputation of the Romans had proceeded them, and the Kush were prepared for conflict. During the 300 hundred years of the Roman occupation of Egypt, they were unable to either conquer or exploit the Kushites, although they tried many times.

As previously mentioned in this text, the Kushites fault several battles with the Romans, most notability the war lead by the Kushite Warrior Queen Amanirenas (Amini-Renas) and her coregent Prince Akinidad. After the death of the Kushite warrior queen, she was succeeded by the

Kandake Amani-shakheto, known as the Scholar Queen. It was Amani-Shakheto that created the new Meroitic script.

To escape the corruptive nature of the Romans, The Kushite moved their capital and their centers of worship deep into Sudan. There was very little friendly interaction between the Romans and the Kush. Meanwhile, the Romans destroyed what was left of the Egyptian culture replacing it with an unconvincing Roman facade.

Twelve Phase of Anu-Egyptian Racial Evolution

By the sixth century AD, the Romans had become irrelevant in north Africa. In approximately 640AD, the Arabs invaded Egypt. After the rapid defeat of the Egyptians, the Arabs migrated from Arabia and the Levant in large numbers. The Arabs settled in the Delta region in the beginning but rapidly moved south beyond the third cataract of the Nile.

The Egyptians, by this time, were little more than a collection of small villages along the Nile River. They were quickly consumed by the Arabs, which represents the last significant racial evolution of the Anu-Egyptians. The Egyptians you see today are the direct descendants of this final racial evolution.

The Arabs expanded across North Africa and were the most powerful militarily force in this region. The Arabs turned their attention to the Kush with an intent to conquer them and spread the religion of Islam. While the Kushites by this time were a fraction of their former selves, they were still the Kush.

When the Arabs invaded Kush, they were able to push the Kush further south. However, the Kush regrouped and were able to repel the Arabs from Kushite lands militarily. The Arabs decided to use a peaceful approach when it came to the Kush, which led to a slow but steady integration of the two cultures.

While many of the Kush remained Christian, the majority eventually accepted Islam. In Sudan today, this dichotomy of Arab Islamic and Black African Christian identity is still alive and well.

Chap 23: The Kushite Cultural Foundation

The Kushite Approach to Identity

Since the beginning of human development, tribes have been struggling with the question of race, religion, culture, nationhood, and identity. The Kushites recognized early in their history that it was not wise to base your identity on things that can easily change. The following narrative will explain why this is true!

Race as the foundation of Identity

Race in the modern age is socially defined by the appearance of a handful of physical characteristics. The ethnic race is a social construct created to give one group a social or economic advantage over another. As previously mentioned, racial traits (phenotype) can be altered with a single mating.

So, what is the race of the offspring of a racial mixture? This question becomes even more profound when you realize that every mating is a mixture of a mix. Humanity has traditionally used race as an excuse to deny their kindship with those who may appear different. This immoral use of the concept of race makes it antithetical to the very meaning of family, tribe, and nation. Why is race antithetical? Because a family, tribe or nation can be made up of many races. The social concept of race has become a weapon used to stereotype, categorize, degrade, attack, and judge others based on appearance.

There is nothing wrong with the concept of race as long as you realize that it has no definitive meaning. Understand, it is not my intent to deny the existence of race or racism. I am merely pointing out the dangerous and destructive hypocrisy underpinning the modern racial concept.

Religion as the Foundation of Identity

There are hundreds of religions practiced on earth. Even religions of the same name are often subdivided into sects or denominations with very different beliefs and practices. Which one of these many religions is the right religion? The answer is simple. My religion! I would argue that even the lack of faith is, in many ways, also a religion.

Religion is an inadequate criterion for an identity for many of the same reasons as race. Faith, like race, when used immorally, is antithetical to the very meaning of family, tribe, and nation. A family, tribe or nation can contain more than one religion, which, if immorally applied, has the potential to divide and destroy the family and social harmony.

Like race, religion can change in the blink of an eye. Religion is also a choice that allows the option of moving from one religion to another. Religion is also evolving, which means it has a tendency to change with time. This tendency to evolve implies that faith can experience a rapid change in tradition, dogma, and practice. Religion can also be used as a weapon to stereotype, categorize, degrade, misjudge, and attack others based on their beliefs.

There is nothing wrong with the concept of religion as long as you realize that it has no definitive meaning. A person can claim to be religious and yet perform extremely evil acts. While a moral theology can mitigate the sins of destructive behavior, it can just as easily be used to justify evil acts. Understand, it is not my intent to ridicule or minimize the importance of faith. I am merely pointing out the dangerous and destructive hypocrisy underpinning the modern concept of religion.

My religious tradition is Christianity. However, it disgusts me to see that Christians in America (U.S.), would accept the banning of Muslims. Is there no room in the collective Christian Inn for Muslims? If not the Muslims, who else will be excluded? Where was the Christian outcry for this immoral banning, especially those who call themselves Christian evangelicals? Given this example, how is any particular religion better as a foundation for identity than any other?

Culture as the Foundation of Identity

Culture is defined as the collective manifestation of human intellectual achievement. The word culture applies to the entire human species. When an individual or group refer to their culture, they are in actuality referring to their subculture. There are thousands of subcultures on planet earth.

The Egyptians, Kushites, Greeks, and Romans were all subcultures within the greater culture that is humankind. Which one of these many subcultures is the right subculture? The answer to this question is almost always simple. My subculture!

Subculture, while incredibly valuable, is still inadequate as a sole source of identity. Subculture, like race and religion, when used immorally, is antithetical to the meaning of family, tribe, and nation. A family can contain more than one subculture. If any given subculture is overemphasized to the exclusion of another, it has the potential to divide and destroy the family and social harmony.

A subculture can also change in the blink of an eye. Subcultures are continually evolving based on contact with other subcultures. This tendency to evolve implies that subcultures can experience a rapid change in tradition and beliefs. Subculture can also be used as a weapon to stereotype, categorize, degrade, attack, and negatively judge others solely because they are not a member or do not identify with the subculture.

There is nothing wrong with the concept of subculture as long as you realize that it has no definitive meaning. While a moral subculture can mitigate destructive behavior, it can also be a catalyst to justify evil. It is not my intent to ridicule or minimize the importance of a subculture. We are all members of one or more subcultures. I am merely pointing out the dangerous and destructive hypocrisy underpinning the concept of a subculture.

Nationalism as the Foundation of Identity

Nationalism is defined as the extreme identification with one's own nation and its interest to the exclusion or detriment of other nations. This source of identity is second only to sexism or racism in its destructive influence on humankind. Nationalism is often motivated by xenophobia, racism, and religious bigotry. Nationalism's propensity to work to the detriment of others makes it both dangerous and divisive as a fundamental source of identity.

There is nothing wrong with being loyal to one's nation and working to the advantage of that nation. We call this very desirable loyalty, patriotism. Patriotism and nationalism are two very different animals. Patriotism works for the good of the society without working to the detriment of its citizens or other countries. The curse of nationalism lay in its propensity to actively work to destroy those who disagree with its self-serving agenda.

The governing type or style of a nation is much less important than the quality of its justice system and its ability to solve national problems <u>justly</u>. The chief goal of nationalism is power. Nationalism measures itself by its ability to project force with no consideration of the morality of its actions. Nationalists believe that it is wealth and military prowess that measures the superiority of a nation, not its morality or the just treatment of its population.

Nationalism is fundamentally flawed and is antithetical to the concept of family, justice, nation or unity. Nationalism is its own worst enemy because it needs an enemy to prosper. Nationalism subverts free well, promotes coercive uniformity, and destroys cooperation throughout the entire world. The enemies of nationalism are both foreign and domestic, making this sense of identity dangerous to everyone.

There is nothing wrong with the concept of patriotism as long as it doesn't become nationalistic. Nationalism is generally immoral, has no definitive meaning, and is a catalyst for injustice. I _do_ ridicule the importance of nationalism as a foundation for identity because it has historically proven itself unfit in a civilized world.

Identity-Based on the Morality

The primary focus of Kushite society was the suppression and destruction of chaos. The Kushites learned early in their civilization that there is only one sense of identity that works for everyone and simultaneously defeats chaos. The Kush discovered that only morality can destroy chaos while promoting goodwill and social harmony. To the Kush, morality, justice, and peace had the same meaning. They understood that without justice, there could be no peace, and without peace, chaos will promote injustice.

Morality is defined as the fundamental principle that establishes the distinction between right and wrong or good and evil behavior. The concept of right and wrong are enigmatic and can be situational and difficult to interpret. However, good and bad behavior is empirical and can be explicitly defined, observed, and measured.

A person's affinity for a (god, culture, race, religion, sex, or nation) may be right or wrong, but it does not measure their devotion to morality. Among the Kush, morality was measured by virtue as it relates to the observable treatment of nature and other human beings. The Kushites believed that any behavior that caused unjust damage to the environment or other human beings was immoral.

Any behavior that induced goodwill, charity, graciousness, inspiration, and virtue in and towards others was Kush (moral). Those who performed destructive or malicious acts towards others without redemption was Apepa (evil or immoral). The Kushites did what few subcultures have ever done. They removed the ambiguity concerning what is right and what is wrong. When I first realized what it really meant to be Kush, I shed tears of shame for my own lack of virtue.

How Kushites Came to This Moral Conclusion

The Kushites realized that laws, traditions, races, religions, and nations change over time. However, the need to combat Chaos did not. The Kushites needed a weapon against Chaos that also did not change, and the Goddess Ma'at provided that weapon. The weapon against chaos is called human virtue. It is also known as morality as defined by the divine code of human decency.

In choosing moral behavior toward others as their testament to morality, the Kushites could avoid humanity's tendency to rationalize immoral behavior. The Kush used the Ma'at as their social guide for acceptable behavior. The Kushite creed also placed the responsibility for moral behavior squarely on the shoulders of the individual.

This ethical approach to identity enabled the Kushite to ignore the superficial and see a person in their full cultural context. They discovered that people of similar values worked wonderfully together and built healthier, more just societies. The wisdom of the Kushite enabled them to appreciate that the real difference between people lay in their fundamental values, not in their traditions, religions, or appearance.

Judge All by the Trilogy-of-Truth

The Kushite trilogy-of-truth was the primary way a Kushite judged themselves and all other human beings. The trilogy assumes that a person's virtue can be examined by observing the consistency in their words and deeds. If a person speaks with balance (justly) yet acts with malice, the Kush would consider that person to be Apepa (evil). The adage, actions speak louder than words is a modern testament to the quality of this philosophical approach. While the trilogy-of-truth may seem simplistic, it has also proven to be extremely accurate.

The Kushites felt that any person who followed the way of the Kush (Ma 'at) was of the Kushite tribe. This virtuous approach to Kushite identity enabled the Kush to more readily accept others, not of their ethnicity, religion, or tradition. The Kush felt that a person could be whoever they happened to be and still follow the moral way of the Kush.

This pragmatic approach to kindship decreased social chaos and promoted harmony among the Kush. The Kushite was interested in the moral quality of the individual. They understood that race, religion, culture, and ethnicity have nothing to do with personal morality, which is what truly defines the quality of a human being. The Kushites were not at all perfect in their behavior, but they humbly strived for redemption.

Kushites Refused to Placate Evil

The secret to forming and sustaining a society based on justice is the absolute refusal of that society to apprise evil and exploitive behavior. The Kushites believed that to appease harmful behavior would invite Chaos and undermine the foundation of your family, tribe, or nation. In my studies, I came upon a Kushite script translated from the Egyptian language. It was written by an unnamed Kushite priest on a wall within the temple of Amun at Jebel Barkal thousands of years ago.

> "To appease Chaos is to feed and strengthen the demon. Give Chaos nothing more than your contempt."

How to Create a Cohesive Society

For a society to endure, it must have a foundation forged in morality. Nothing is more critical to social cohesiveness and harmony than the virtue of its people. Justice is the only soil upon which a great and moral society can grow. Justice, not wealth, must be the priority of your nation or it will eat itself alive. Peace and true prosperity can only be achieved through justice and social balance. If your nation lacks a moral foundation, it will eventually crumble into the arms of Chaos.

The Kushites realized that the process of creating a harmonious society would be complicated, especially if the culture is diverse. But it can be done with perseverance and the unwavering devotion to a moral vision. You must set aside the curse of the uncaring (lack of empathy) and embrace virtue as the only antidote to personal and social turmoil. While there are many paths in life, the way of the Kush is the only one that leads to peace!

Chapter 24 – A Gift to the Diasporic Kushite

Kushite Doctrine of Human Decency

A diasporic Kushite is a moral human being who understands and accepts the Kushite code of human decency. The diasporic Kushite has an unwavering need for social harmony and a boundless craving for justice. The diasporic Kushite has a transcending spirit and a deep-seated need to create a just, well-balanced, ethical, and empathetic world.

The diasporic Kushite is respectful and a friend to all things human except (chaos). The diasporic Kushite transcends race, creed, and ideology while accepting the unfortunate imperfections that drive our species. Most importantly, the diasporic Kushite is a courageous human being who refuses to excuse or placate evil, including the evil that lurks within ourselves.

It's Time to Take a Stand

For too long, we, the diasporic Kushite, have allowed those with corrosively bias world views to interpret the histories of those they have victimized. The fields of anthropology, archaeology, and Egyptology are dominated by a culture that has historically believed that people of color were less than human. This same culture thought that women were biologically, spiritually, and intellectually inferior to men. How foolish would it be to allow this same moral deviancy to interpret your history, philosophy, and most importantly, your interpretation of oneself?

My Bias Interpretation of History

I am not an Egyptologist, Anthropologist, or Archaeologist. But I'm also not a complete idiot, despite my deficits! I understand and rejoice in the potential of all of humanity. In this text, I have attempted to show you a history that few others are aware of or would dare to expose. Even fewer understand the significance of this historical interpretation and its profound effect on those who are made aware of it.

Western cultures have barely discovered the history of the Kushites. They completely fail to understand the historical relationship between the Kush and the Kemet. Yet, they comfortably claim that the Egyptians dominated the Kush. Why would a statement of dominance have any historical relevance? The answer is simple. The need to address authority is a characteristic of those harboring a deep-seated cultural inferiority complex. Unfortunately, we the African diaspora have been forced to carry the humiliating consequences of another culture's inferiority complex.

In this text, I have addressed the historical questions that failed to be asked about the Kushite and Kemet civilizations. For example, how were the Kushites and Kemet related? Who were the original people of Kemet? How did the racial evolution of Kemet occur? What is the moral relevance of the Ma 'at to both cultures? Could the Ma 'at the possible origin of the ten commandments?

The above questions are just a few of the remarkable cultural revelations offered in this text and are critically important to the African diaspora's future psychological development. I believe that my bias interpretation of the evidence has just as much merit, if not more, than those who have and would deny our humanity.

The Ramification of Cultural Genocide

Those who were kidnapped and held hostage in the new world have had our humanity systemically destroyed by the slaver and Jim Crow law. We are the victims of a human atrocity that must be culturally rectified. Unfortunately for the slaver and their decedents, they do not possess the will or moral capability to correct this wrong without our firm and unrelenting guidance.

The power to remedy the cultural damage caused by colonialism and slavery is in the victims' hands. It is our responsibility to right this wrong, and it begins with taking command of our collective cultural history. How you perceive yourself through the lens of history has the potential to unleash that which was denied. This Kushite history is just one among many African histories that will wrench back your self-respect, confidence, critical thinking, and imagination, enabling you to build a better future in your own image.

It Won't Change Until We Change it!

I have read countless books about Egypt and the Kush. Some of these texts were written by the most exceptional scientists in their fields. Despite their experience, education, and the evidence, they remain blind to the historical contributions of those not of their tribe.

In this text, I have taken a bold step in presenting to you an alternative history of one of the oldest civilizations on earth. My goal was to show you that black people were and still are the origin of civilization. It was we who discovered in antiquity that civilization is not defined by buildings or aqueducks, but by how we treat our fellow human beings.

When confronted with my historical proposition, western academia puckers like an inflamed hemorrhoid. They immediately become defensive, condescending, and factually manipulative. Where is your PhD? They ask with contempt. I humbly reply with the question, where is your morality?

While these scientists do an outstanding job finding historical evidence, you cannot trust their culturally biased interpretation of the evidence they find. I chose to focus on Egypt and the Kush because, in so many ways, the race-based culture wars began in this place and time. The stories told in this text are a prime example of why my historical declarations are <u>probably</u> much closer to the truth regarding the history of the ancient land of Kemet. If am correct, then consider all of the other historic lies told sense this ancient time that must be rectified.

The Cultural Gifts of the Great Kush

The Kushites went to great lengths to ensure that they would never be forgotten. This African ancestor wanted you to know that they built the pyramids, created language, fought just wars, forged a moral civilization, and struggled to keep their ideas alive. The Anu-Kush built temples, deffufas, palaces, sculptures, and art. The Anu-Kush was also arguably the cultural origin of the written word.

The Kushites held to their traditions and traded their goods with the ancient known world. The Kush contemplated, explored, and discovered the truth about humanity's nature, loved, and ceremoniously buried their dead. The Anu-Kush fought and defeated all parasitic civilizations, preventing them from taking our motherland and enslaving its people in antiquity. Now imagine what horrors would have confronted black people if there were no Kush.

The Anu-Kush choose to build their society on a foundation of morality instead of greed and dominance. This alone makes them the greatest people I have ever known. The Kushite has enabled us to see who we really are and to recognize the righteous path to what we can become. The incredible gifts bestowed upon us by this African ancestor deserves nothing less than our unwavering respect. We honor the Kushite by never allowing their name and the divine meaning of that name to be erased from humankind's memory!

Kushite Continuity-of-Self

Understanding the Ma 'at and Kushite history is the greatest gift a culture could bestow upon the African diaspora. It is the single only way you can once again acquire complete continuity-of-self. Continuity-of-self is the unbroken and contiguous view of one's existence through the lens of our ancient ancestors. It is a form of spiritual and ethnic manna that feeds the very soul of our humanity.

All of us need to know and understand the true history that represents our collective tribe. No other culture on earth has more honorably served African people's essence than the Kushite (the moral human being).

Recall the Kushite concept of self-possession. Self-possession is a state of mind. It implies that you know who you are, what you are, and why you exist. Self-possession is not only a powerful psychological state of mind; it's also essential to your success as a human being. Without self-possession, there can be no genuine acceptance of self.

Without self-acceptance, there is no pathway to identity, kindship, and cultural continuity. Without the Kush, you have, at best, a partial historical foundation upon which to build your future. While a partial historical foundation can work for the strongest among us, it will fail the common. If there is no historically factual foundation, there is no platform upon which to take a moral stand in your own name.

Self-possession enables you to build the moral character and courage required to forge an independent future. For without the courage to form an autonomous future, you are little more than a slave.

Kushite Craving for Justice

Most people have a sense of justice, or at least we did as children. If you are a parent with two or more children, you may have experienced what some call the child comparison wars. A comparison war occurs when you inadvertently give more to one child than the other. The child who receives less will immediately notice and may loudly complain.

All children have a natural sense of entitlement when it comes to justice, and there is absolutely nothing wrong with this. Every person is entitled to fairness! The need to experience justice for one's self is the beginning step on the road to building a moral human being. The key is to teach the child to expand their sense of justice beyond self. Justice can be instilled by teaching the child the meaning and importance of the golden gene, empathy. The Kush believed that a person without empathy beyond self was profoundly flawed and completely incapable of just leadership. The worlds recent experience with Donald Trump has proven the Kushites correct.

An Enlighten Kushite Diaspora

There are many diverse members of the Kushite diaspora, and not all have had the same experience with evil. Today, the diaspora is exceptionally varied and exists throughout the world. The modern diaspora speaks many languages and may have its own sense of identity, customs, faith, and tradition. This new diaspora is the product of immigration, forced or otherwise, and may feel estranged from their ancient ancestors. This level of diversity can only be overcome by accepting the way of the Kush.

The Kushite method of assimilation allows a person to choose whatever ethnicity to which they relate, and still remain Kush. Your external self matters little to the Kushite because it is your virtue that we seek. The Kushite wants to know if you are Apepa, or are you Kush? But no matter who you are, the Kush will judge you according to the trilogy-of-truth.

Those of African heritage have a special relationship with the way of the Kush. It was from the essence of African people that this beautiful concept arose. Because the Ma 'at has its origin in the motherland, it should be more attractive to our African kindred. However, the real mission of the Ma 'at is to bind people based on morality rather than heritage. Regardless of ethnicity, to be Kush is to speak and behave in a manner compatible with the code of human decency.

Law and Order is no Substitute for Justice.

Another ancient lesson given to the diaspora by the Kush is that realization that law and order is no substitute for justice. The lack of justice is the root cause of all social problems plaguing societies around the world. The Kushites realized the imperative of understanding the differences between law, order, and justice. The only statute that is valid in the mind of a Kushite is the law that is both morally and consistently applied. Break this moral imperative, and you invite social disorder, poverty, and conflict.

No Kushite is obligated to follow an immoral law and, in fact, should resist it. When a law is unjust or unfairly applied, it ceases to be just and becomes little more than coercion. Unfair statutes applied unjustly will lead to devastating social consequences, including violence, disunity, and a fracturing of national identity.

While a superficial calm can be temporarily achieved using violence, the order will be short-lived. History has shown that the violence that returns will be more brutal due to the perceived injustice inherent in the violent suppression. Violence also assures an eventual violent response, cascading into chaos. If an opponent is seeking **dominance** via violence rather than justice, you have identified the source of the problem.

Harmony cannot be achieved by force or by injustice. Injustice is antithetical to peace, so force and peace cannot coexist. The more force you add to a situation, the more likely the strategy will result in turmoil. You must balance law, order, and punishment with a moral consistency, or you will never enjoy lasting peace.

Injustice may seem passive-aggressive, but in reality, it is no less brutal a form of violence than is a sharp blow to the head. The diasporic Kush should try to use words to make the enemy understand the brutal ramifications of injustice. If words go unheeded, then war must ensue. Given this, the Kushite will make war until the unjust attacks stop, and the damage is rectified. Every just war fought by the Kush was a last resort effort to crush an injustice. The enemy must be made to understand that the responsibility for peace lay on the shoulders of all humanity and is rooted in cooperation.

The Gods Do Exist!

The Kushite is the child of Amun and the original human being. You may substitute the name of your God in place of Amun because it makes no difference to a Kushite. The God Amun promised the Kush that as they were first, so shall they be the last to past from this earth. No matter what the fate of the original Kushite nation, the Kush would rise again in the form of a robust global diaspora. There will come to past a new Kushite race of many races, whose righteousness in the face of evil will elevate them to the guardians of social justice.

When the diaspora rises, the lords of Chaos will scatter like startled birds as they witness with confusion the unstoppable rise of the new Kushite. When the moral human being accepts the way of the Kush, they will mercilessly destroy the lies that have fuel disunity and Chaos among all of humankind. More importantly, the Diasporic Kushite has the power to bring back to the consciousness of humanity, the profound relevance of the Code of Human Decency.

Emulate the Kush!

The Kushite diaspora needs to emulate something! So why not follow the best of who you already are. When I was a child, I sought an identity beyond that provided by the colonialist. I was lucky to have found the Kush. The knowledge of the Kush enabled me to understand the world and become a positive contributor to it. The Kushites were the only culture I could find that met _my_ stringent criteria which included these social characteristics:

A society based on morality, not greed.
Respect and admiration for women.
Respect for human dignity.
Socially just.
Socially progressive.
Proven longevity.
Morality based religion.
Linguistic genius.
Representational government.
Complex social structure.
Physically diverse population.
Morality based behavioral system.
A military tradition.
Will not hesitate to fight a just war.
Refuses to placate evil.
A willingness to kick-ass to defend self, family and justice.

I believe that the way of the Kush is the only path to social harmony and a reasonable option for the future of humanity. Without the clarity of the past, there can be no definitive vision of the future. The world is in great need of a 21st century Kushite, and you the Diasporic Kushite are it.

Accepting the way of the Kush is our collective destiny. Without such an approach, humankind will in time cease to exist. As the black African female oracles of antiquity once stated, "If we forsake one another, the gods will forsake us all!"

Made in the USA
Las Vegas, NV
26 February 2021